Canadian Daily Language Activities

—— Grade 5 ——

Written by Eleanor M. Summers

Our Canadian Daily Language Activities series provides short and quick opportunities for students to review and reinforce skills in punctuation, grammar, spelling, language and reading comprehension. The Bonus Activities that follow each week of skills are fun tasks such as word and vocabulary puzzles, figurative language and reading exercises. A short interesting fact about Canada is the finishing touch!

ELEANOR M. SUMMERS is a retired teacher who is still actively involved in education. She has created many resources in language, science and history. As a writer, she enjoys creating practical and thought-provoking resources for teachers and parents.

Copyright © On The Mark Press 2016

This publication may be reproduced under licence from Access Copyright, or with the express written permission of On The Mark Press, or as permitted by law. All rights are otherwise reserved, and no part of this publication may be reproduced, stored in a retrieval system, or transmitted in any form or by any means, electronic, mechanical, photocopying, scanning, recording or otherwise, except as specifically authorized.

All Rights Reserved.
Printed in Canada.

Published in Canada by:
On The Mark Press
15 Dairy Avenue, Napanee, Ontario, K7R 1M4
www.onthemarkpress.com

#OTM2148

Topics cover:
Properties of and Changes in Matter, Chemistry in the Classroom; Forces and Simple Machines; Forces Acting on Structures and Mechanisms; Mechanisms Using Electricity; and Electricity and Magnetism.

#OTM2156

Topics cover:
Conservation of Energy, Renewable and Non-Renewable Resources and Weather.

This series includes learning intentions, goals, success criteria suggestions, topic resources, a vocabulary list, detailed lesson plans, student resources, and additional web based resources, answer keys, ideas for differentiation, accommodations, enrichment and extension activities. Each unit can be used as a whole to fulfill the overall expectation requirements for this curriculum or it can be used by activity to compliment other resources and activities.

#J1111

#J1110

HOW TO USE: CANADIAN DAILY LANGUAGE ACTIVITIES

This book is divided into 32 weekly sections.

Each weekly section provides daily skill review and assessment activities.

ACTIVITIES 1 – 4

Focus is on:

- punctuation, capitalization, grammar, and spelling
- language and reading comprehension skills

ACTIVITY 5

Focus is on:

- a single language or reading skill

BONUS ACTIVITY

Provides opportunities for extended activities.

- word puzzles, vocabulary development
- spelling
- reading skills
- includes a short, interesting fact about Canada

STUDENT PROGRESS CHART

- Students record their daily score for each Language Activity.
- At the end of the week, they calculate their Total Score
- At the end of four weeks, students evaluate their performance.
- Students will require one copy of page 3 and three copies of page 4 to record results for entire 32 weeks. Teachers may wish to make back-to-back copies.

TEACHER SUGGESTIONS

- All activities may be completed for each week or teachers may exclude some.
- New skills may be completed as a whole class activity.
- Bonus Activities may be used at teachers' discretion.
- Correcting student work together will help model the correct responses.
- Monitor student mastery of skills from information on the Student Progress Chart.

PROGRESS CHART

How many did you get correct each day? Record your score on the chart.

Week	Activity 1	Activity 2	Activity 3	Activity 4	Activity 5	Total Score
#	/5	/5	/5	/5	/5	/25

Week	Activity 1	Activity 2	Activity 3	Activity 4	Activity 5	Total Score
#	/5	/5	/5	/5	/5	/25

Week	Activity 1	Activity 2	Activity 3	Activity 4	Activity 5	Total Score
#	/5	/5	/5	/5	/5	/25

Week	Activity 1	Activity 2	Activity 3	Activity 4	Activity 5	Total Score
#	/5	/5	/5	/5	/5	/25

My strongest skills are _____

My skills that need improvement are _____

The Bonus Activities I liked best are _____

Week	Activity 1	Activity 2	Activity 3	Activity 4	Activity 5	Total Score
#	/5	/5	/5	/5	/5	/25

Week	Activity 1	Activity 2	Activity 3	Activity 4	Activity 5	Total Score
#	/5	/5	/5	/5	/5	/25

Week	Activity 1	Activity 2	Activity 3	Activity 4	Activity 5	Total Score
#	/5	/5	/5	/5	/5	/25

Week	Activity 1	Activity 2	Activity 3	Activity 4	Activity 5	Total Score
#	/5	/5	/5	/5	/5	/25

My strongest skills are _____

My skills that need improvement are _____

The Bonus Activities I liked best are _____

Week	Activity 1	Activity 2	Activity 3	Activity 4	Activity 5	Total Score
#	/5	/5	/5	/5	/5	/25

Week	Activity 1	Activity 2	Activity 3	Activity 4	Activity 5	Total Score
#	/5	/5	/5	/5	/5	/25

Week	Activity 1	Activity 2	Activity 3	Activity 4	Activity 5	Total Score
#	/5	/5	/5	/5	/5	/25

Week	Activity 1	Activity 2	Activity 3	Activity 4	Activity 5	Total Score
#	/5	/5	/5	/5	/5	/25

My strongest skills are _____

My skills that need improvement are _____

The Bonus Activities I liked best are _____

Week	Activity 1	Activity 2	Activity 3	Activity 4	Activity 5	Total Score
#	/5	/5	/5	/5	/5	/25

Week	Activity 1	Activity 2	Activity 3	Activity 4	Activity 5	Total Score
#	/5	/5	/5	/5	/5	/25

Week	Activity 1	Activity 2	Activity 3	Activity 4	Activity 5	Total Score
#	/5	/5	/5	/5	/5	/25

Week	Activity 1	Activity 2	Activity 3	Activity 4	Activity 5	Total Score
#	/5	/5	/5	/5	/5	/25

My strongest skills are _____

My skills that need improvement are _____

The Bonus Activities I liked best are _____

DAILY LANGUAGE ACTIVITIES SKILLS LIST

This book provides many opportunities for practice of the following skills:

Vocabulary & Word Skills
- word meaning from context
- root words/prefixes/suffixes
- vowel sounds
- spelling
- syllabication
- synonyms/antonyms/homonyms
- contractions

Capitalization
- beginning of sentences
- proper names/titles of people
- names of places
- titles of books, songs, poems
- names of days, months, holidays
- abbreviations

Punctuation
- punctuation at the end of a sentence
- commas in a series
- commas in dates and addresses
- commas in compound sentences
- commas in simple dialogue
- commas after an introductory phrase/clause
- commas in direct address/parenthetical expressions
- commas after appositives
- commas between adjectives
- periods in abbreviations/initials
- use of colons
- quotation marks in speech
- quotation marks: poems, songs, stories
- apostrophes in contractions
- apostrophes in possessives
- interjections
- punctuation in a friendly letter
- run on sentences
- underlining: books, plays, poems, magazines

Grammar & Word Usage
- subject and object pronouns
- common/proper nouns
- singular/plural nouns
- possessive nouns
- verb forms
- verb tenses
- double negatives
- adjectives
- adverbs
- correct article/determiner/adjective/adverb
- parts of speech
- comparative/superlative
- subject/predicate
- subject – verb agreement
- prepositional phrases
- sentence types
- sentence combinations

Reading Comprehension
- analogies
- categorization
- cause and effect
- fact or opinion
- fact or fantasy
- fiction or nonfiction
- figurative language
- inference
- simile/metaphor
- idioms, proverbs

Reference Skills
- alphabetical order
- dictionary skills
- reference materials
- media sources

Name: _____

WEEK 1

Correct these sentences.

1. we don't gots no snow in hour yard yet
   _____

2. my sister amy will say her speech at the royal canadian legion contest
   _____

ACTIVITY 1

TOTAL /5

Fact or fiction?

3. Snow falls in every part of Canada. _____

4. The snowman did a fancy dance for the children. _____

Use context clues to explain the underlined word.

5. <u>Catastrophes</u>, like flooding and tornadoes, may be caused by extreme weather.
   _____

Name: _____

WEEK 1

Write the best word to complete this sentence.

1. I _____ have any money to buy a treat.   **doesn't / wasn't / don't / isn't**

Correct these sentences.

2. i red an amazing adventure story about vikings visiting north america long ago
   _____

3. one explorer named leif the lucky may have settled in newfoundland
   _____

ACTIVITY 2

TOTAL /5

Common or proper noun?

4. Moose Factory   _____

5. monarch butterfly   _____

SSR1148   ISBN: 9781771587341 © On The Mark Press

7

Name: _____

What reference source would you use to find:

WEEK 1
ACTIVITY 3
TOTAL /5

1. an synonym for "hungry"   _____

2. the location of James Bay   _____

Correct these sentences.

3. our family is gonna visit the dinosaur display at the royal ontario museum
   _____

4. wouldnt it be fun to watch wales play in the waters of the atlantic ocean
   _____

Complete this analogy.

5. pilot is to airplane as jockey is to _____

Name: _____

Divide each word into syllables.

WEEK 1
ACTIVITY 4
TOTAL /5

1. snowboarding   _____

2. Fredericton   _____

Correct these sentences.

3. have you ever scene a double reinbow in the sky asked alan
   _____

4. i has read most of the adventure books written by pierre berton
   _____

Where would you find this part of a friendly letter?

5. Your friend, Clint   _____

Name: _____

WEEK 1

ACTIVITY 5

TOTAL /5

Explain the meaning of the underlined expressions.

1. Becky <u>had high hopes</u> that she would win the contest.
   _____

2. Aaron hoped he could <u>win over</u> his mother to let him go scuba diving.
   _____

3. Not a creature <u>was stirring</u>, not even my cat!
   _____

4. Mr. Green <u>has the best head</u> for planning track and field events.
   _____

5. The adventurers <u>took to the road</u> without a care.
   _____

Name: _____

WEEK 1

Bonus Activity   Where Am I?

Where would you find each one of these? Draw a line to connect your answers.

1. The Rocky Mountains   Nova Scotia
2. Canada's Parliament Buildings   Saskatchewan
3. Red soil and fields of potatoes British Columbia
4. The Calgary Stampede   Newfoundland
5. Bonhomme   Ontario
6. The city of Winnipeg   New Brunswick
7. Grain elevators   Prince Edward Island
8. The Magnetic Hill   Manitoba
9. The harbour of Halifax   Alberta
10. A moose strolling along the highway   Québec

MY CANADA

The Canada Bank Note Company in Ottawa, printed the last Canadian one-dollar bill on April 20, 1989.

Name: _____

Correct these sentences.

1. on may 20 2015 my brother rick will graduate from mcgill university
   _____

2. is you gonna help me with hour report on first nations ceremonies
   _____

Write the past tense of these verbs.

3. carry   _____

4. grow   _____

Synonym or antonym?

5. seldom, often _____

WEEK 2
ACTIVITY 1
TOTAL /5

Name: _____

Write the predicate of this sentence.

1. The graceful deer jumped over the fence with ease.
   _____

Fact or fiction?

2. Canada exports oil to other countries.   _____

3. An icebreaker never gets trapped in the ice. _____

Correct these sentences.

4. mom maid chocolit chip cookies and we eight them all
   _____

5. how good did you due on your math test nigel asked
   _____

WEEK 2
ACTIVITY 2
TOTAL /5

Name: _____

Write the root word (base word) for:

1. unremarkable _____

Correct these sentences.

2. a teem of workers is trying to find treasure on oak island
_____

3. we is reading the poem the train dogs by e pauline johnson
_____

What do the words in each group have in common?

4. poutine, beaver tail, snow cone _____

5. Erie, Ontario, Huron, Superior, Michigan _____

WEEK 2
ACTIVITY 3
TOTAL /5

Name: _____

Correct these sentences.

1. im going to edmonton nest weak to sea my cousen brady
_____

2. due you think you could ride a hoarse without a saddle asked rex
_____

Underline the word that comes last in alphabetical order.

3. waist   women   write   wrote   wrong

4. sign   saga   scenery   shoemaker   swim

Write a common noun for this proper noun.

5. Raptors _____

WEEK 2
ACTIVITY 4
TOTAL /5

Name: _____

Reference sources: atlas, almanac, dictionary, encyclopedia, thesaurus

What reference source would be best to look for information on the following:

1. the location of the Prince Charles Island _____
2. a antonym for the word "generous" _____
3. the biggest city in Canada _____
4. the meaning of the word "global" _____
5. the foods eaten by the caribou _____

WEEK 2
ACTIVITY 5
TOTAL /5

Name: _____

Bonus Activity: Just for Fun: Anagrams

Change the order of the letters in each underlined word to make the correct word to match the clue.

1. Change mean into hair on a horse or a lion. _____
2. Change snail into things we hammer. _____
3. Change snoop into something you use when you eat soup. _____
4. Change blow into something that could hold cereal. _____
5. Change hubs into a small shrub. _____
6. Change paws into a stinging insect. _____
7. Change wand into a word meaning daybreak. _____
8. Change cork into a word meaning stone. _____

WEEK 2
BONUS ACTIVITY

Sam Steele was a respected Mountie who kept law and order during the rowdy Klondike Gold Rush. People called him the "Lion of the Yukon".

MY CANADA

Name: _____

WEEK 3 — ACTIVITY 1 — TOTAL /5

Correct these sentences.

1. i had mustard relish ketchup and onions on my hot dog said connie
   _____

2. this peace of pizza has two much pepperoni and it is to hot too eat
   _____

Write two words that rhyme with:

3. tough _____

4. dawn _____

Fiction or nonfiction?

5. If you catch a leprechaun, he will lead you to a pot of gold. _____

Name: _____

WEEK 3 — ACTIVITY 2 — TOTAL /5

Complete these analogies.

1. Car is to street as train is to _____

2. Bear is to fur as fish is to _____

Correct these sentences.

3. us laughed when we heard the story called how the bear got his short tail
   _____

4. the canadian armed forces is very brave men and womin
   _____

Fact or opinion.

5. Girls look better with long hair. _____

Name: _____

WEEK 3 — ACTIVITY 3 — TOTAL /5

What do these words have in common?

1. Charlottetown, Regina, Edmonton, Toronto _____

2. chocolate chip, sugar, gingersnap, wafer _____

Correct these sentences.

3. befour you go to bed take a bath and brush youre teeth
   _____

4. dont walk on the cleen floor with them derty books said mom
   _____

Give the past tense of this verb.

5. sink _____

Name: _____

WEEK 3 — ACTIVITY 4 — TOTAL /5

Tell if the underlined word is a *noun, verb, adjective* or *adverb*.

1. We made <u>snow</u> sculptures from all that packy snow. _____

2. Strong winds <u>whipped</u> the snow into huge banks for sliding. _____

Correct these sentences.

3. we is going to big cheese for my birthday party on saturday
   _____

4. i wants to joine the royal canadian mounted police when i is older
   _____

Fact or opinion?

5. Hot oatmeal is the best breakfast on a cold winter day. _____

Name: _____

Combine these sentences to make one good sentence.

WEEK 3
ACTIVITY 5
TOTAL /5

1. We travelled to the city. We drove our van. The trip took two hours.
   _____

2. Danny can run fast. He wins races all the time. He beats older kids too.
   _____

3. Ellie fell off her bike. She scraped her knee. Mom put a band-aid on it.
   _____

4. This store is going out of business. Everything is on sale. I want new basketball shoes.
   _____

5. Dad is painting my bedroom. He is painting it green. I picked the colour.
   _____

Name: _____

Bonus Activity: Rhyming Words

WEEK 3
BONUS ACTIVITY

One word in each sentence is not right. Underline the incorrect word. Then write a correct word that rhymes with the underlined one

1. You coil water before making tea.   _____

2. We had a meal of dish and chips.   _____

3. The ship hit a coral beef.   _____

4. Jennie washed her face and hands with rope.   _____

5. Juan swam in the turf.   _____

6. You should be careful hiding your bike in the traffic.   _____

MY CANADA Halifax was founded in 1749. Its motto is: Riches from the Sea. People who live there are called Haligonians.

Name: _____

Correct these sentences.

1. my parents went to the golden dragon for there anniversary
   _____

2. prof e m johnson is going to be teaching the course that starts on january 16 2015
   _____

Tell if the comma is used correctly.

3. 192, Pineview Drive   _____

4. Nov. 11, 1918   _____

What part of speech is the underlined word: *noun, verb, adverb* **or** *adjective.*

5. We are going to Mensen's Farm to <u>pick</u> strawberries. _____

WEEK 4
ACTIVITY 1
TOTAL /5

Name: _____

Underline the adjectives in this sentence.

1. The ragged little boy was begging for any tiny scrap of food.

Write the plural form of each noun.

2. life   _____

3. sheep   _____

Correct these sentences.

4. ill get me and you an ice creem coon for a treet said callie
   _____

5. wow thats a great time for yur first run said coach barrett
   _____

WEEK 4
ACTIVITY 2
TOTAL /5

Name: _____

Complete the analogies.

1. Foot is to sock as head is to _____

2. Beard is to chin as moustache is to _____

Correct these sentences.

3. dont weight two long to by your ticket to the big game
   _____

4. why ain't you goin with me and my brother eric
   _____

Underline the adverbs in this sentence.

5. A ninja breathes softly, moves silently and attacks quickly.

WEEK 4
ACTIVITY 3
TOTAL /5

Name: _____

Subject or object pronoun?

1. Dad took Hannah and <u>me</u> to the beach. _____

2. She said that she would pick <u>it</u> up for me. _____

Correct these sentences.

3. their are for baby ducks swimmed in the pond in the park
   _____

4. doesnt there mother do a good job of keepin them safe frum enemies
   _____

Circle the correct abbreviation for Prince Edward Island.

5.   PEI   PrEdIs   P.E.I   PE Island

WEEK 4
ACTIVITY 4
TOTAL /5

Name: _____

Choose the best word to complete each sentence.

1. If we play _____ at the practice today, we may make the team.
   well / good / best

2. Jean and _____ have signed up for Library Helper Club.
   I / me / us

3. Did James have a _____ time on his trip to Vancouver?
   well / good / best

4. _____ apple pie is the best I have ever tasted!
   Them / Those / That

5. Please help _____ cross the busy street.
   she / her / I

WEEK 4
ACTIVITY 5
TOTAL /5

Name: _____

Bonus Activity: Antonyms

Solve the puzzle by filling in the correct *antonym* for each word clue. Write one letter in each box. Your answer must have the correct number of letters.

more								
soft								
full								
over								
together								
inner								
rough								
after								
sunny								
crooked								
forward								
safe								

WEEK 4

The *moose population* in Newfoundland and Labrador is higher than anywhere else in North America... more than 150, 000 in total!

MY CANADA

Name: _____

Fact or fantasy?

1. Harry Potter battled with many enemies and won. _____

Correct these sentences.

2. the scaryest book i has ever read is called into the dark waters

   _____

3. jeffrey hopes to travel to many countrys in the world especially in asia and europe

   _____

Give the possessive pronoun.

4. the colours of the dresses   _____

5. the truck of Duke   _____

WEEK 5

ACTIVITY 1

TOTAL /5

Name: _____

Circle the preposition in each sentence.

1. Jack stood beside his brother at the ceremony.
2. They are building a new house near the lake.

Correct these sentences.

3. children need to bee protected aganst measles mumps and chickenpocks

   _____

4. maddie will you help me clean out the old attic asked grandma

   _____

Give your opinion of the following topic.

5. skiing down a big hill _____

WEEK 5

ACTIVITY 2

TOTAL /5

Name: _____

WEEK 5 — ACTIVITY 3

Explain the meaning of the underlined figure of speech.

1. They <u>were all moved</u> by his story. _____

2. Don't <u>make mountains out of molehills</u>. _____

Write the root word for:

3. population _____

Correct these sentences.

4. if you dont help him with his math no more he will get upset
   _____

5. did there knew winter coates all costed the same amount of money
   _____

TOTAL /5

Name: _____

WEEK 5 — ACTIVITY 4

Fact or fiction?

1. Frozen precipitation might be in the form of hail. _____

Correct these sentences.

2. the wilsons asked noreen to sing at there daughters wedding in june
   _____

3. nathan has did his spellin work correct and so has me
   _____

What reference source would you use to find out:

4. the weather for the coming week _____

5. the location of the Ottawa River _____

TOTAL /5

Name: _____

Decide if the underlined parts have a *capitalization error*, a *punctuation error*, a *spelling error* or *no mistake*.

WEEK 5
ACTIVITY 5
TOTAL /5

1. <u>monarch</u> butterflies are beautiful creatures. _____

2. We can easily recognize them <u>by their black and orange colours</u>. _____

3. Have you ever seen them when they start to swarm <u>in the fall</u> _____

4. They are preparing for their long journey <u>to mexico</u>. _____

5. They will <u>retern</u> in the spring to start a new life cycle. _____

Name: _____

Bonus Activity: On the Open Seas!

WEEK 5

Unscramble these words to make the names of water craft. Use the clues in the picture to help you.

1. karnte _____
2. pish _____
3. frat _____
4. ocean _____
5. chaty _____
6. seiucr phis _____
7. alsobait _____
8. brainmuse _____

Great Slave Lake, in Northwest Territories, is the deepest lake in North America. Its depth is 614 metres!

MY CANADA

Name: _____

WEEK 6 — ACTIVITY 1

Correct these sentences.

1. who think that canada owns the north pole asked the teacher
   _____

2. i thought the poler bares owned it joked owen
   _____

TOTAL /5

Circle the adjectives in each sentence.

3. The cranky old man kept the boy's rubber ball that went through the wire fence.

4. Put the small jars of blueberry jam on the top shelf in the big pantry.

Use context clues to explain the meaning of the underlined word.

5. The pioneers would kill deer in the fall to have enough <u>venison</u> for the long winter.
   _____

Name: _____

WEEK 6 — ACTIVITY 2

Write the comparative and superlative form of this adjective.

1. dusty   _____   _____

What is this person probably doing?

2. Mom got out her cookbook and turned to her favourite recipe. Then she gathered all the ingredients. _____

3. I listened for the coach to say,"On your mark. Get set. Go!"
   _____

TOTAL /5

Correct these sentences.

4. him and jason wanted to see the knew models at the international auto show
   _____

5. why dont you play quiet while your baby brother stewie is napping
   _____

Name: _____

Tell if this sentence is *declarative, interrogative, imperative* or *exclamatory*.

1. Pick up all your toys and wash your hands before dinner.
   _____

Give your opinion about each topic.

2. travelling by dogsled _____

3. paddling a canoe _____

Correct these sentences.

4. why did them dear come so neer to grampa bobs cabin
   _____

5. we has swum in lake ontario sevan times in the passed year
   _____

WEEK 6
ACTIVITY 3
TOTAL /5

- -

Name: _____

Correct these sentences.

1. is we gonna go skateboarding with there group on friday
   _____

2. her and me go for hour skating lesson each tuesday at 330
   _____

Is the underlined word a common noun or a proper noun?

3. The <u>rider</u> of the horse encouraged it to jump over the highest rail.
   _____

4. <u>Big Ben</u>, a champion jumper, easily cleared the bar. _____

Write one sentence using this pair of homonyms: kernel, colonel

5. _____

WEEK 6
ACTIVITY 4
TOTAL /5

SSR1148   ISBN: 9781771587341 © On The Mark Press   23

Name: _____

Explain the meaning of the underlined figures of speech.

WEEK 6
ACTIVITY 5
TOTAL /5

1. Wait a minute. It's <u>right on the tip of my tongue</u>.
   _____

2. We will <u>leave no stone unturned</u> to find your money.
   _____

3. Winning that prize put Crystal <u>on top of the world</u>.
   _____

4. Sometimes you <u>drive me up the wall</u>.
   _____

5. And you <u>give me a splitting headache</u>!
   _____

Name: _____

Bonus Activity: Words from Native Languages

WEEK 6

Prepositions are words that begin a *group of words* known as *phrases*. Choose a preposition from the Word Box to complete each sentence.

1. Frank and Marie went skateboarding _____ the park.
2. Frank was going too fast and fell _____ his skateboard.
3. Marie saw what happened and rushed _____ to help him.
4. Frank wasn't hurt badly, just a few cuts _____ his legs.
5. Marie walked home _____ Frank to make him feel better.
6. Frank put his skateboard _____ his bed.
7. _____ a few days he decided to try again.

Word Box: in, under, over, on, with, off, after, for, into

MY CANADA
In Quebec City, you can spend a winter night in a hotel completely made of ice. It is the first *ice hotel* in North America.

Name: _____

Correct these sentences.

1. claires dog buddy waggs its tale when it like you

   _____

2. do you no who teared the pages of my libary book asked chris

   _____

Give the past tense of these verbs

3. sweep   _____

4. blow   _____

Use context clues to determine the meaning of the underlined word.

5. Robinson Crusoe was very lonely after being <u>marooned</u> on an island.

   _____

WEEK 7
ACTIVITY 1
TOTAL /5

Name: _____

Write a proper noun for the following common nouns.

1. mystery television show   _____

2. playground game   _____

Where would the following probably take place?

3. The Northern Lights made a spectacular show in the sky.

   _____

Correct these sentences.

4. it dont make no difference if you helps me with this boaring job

   _____

5. mom scolded me you should have ben more carful with your knew shoos

   _____

WEEK 7
ACTIVITY 2
TOTAL /5

Name: _____

WEEK 7
ACTIVITY 3
TOTAL /5

Subject pronoun or object pronoun?

1. Is <u>she</u> ready to play the game? _____

Correct these sentences.

2. youll need flower suger butter chocolate chips and eggs to make those cookys
   _____

3. do you beleive that ice skating is won of the most poplar sports in canada
   _____

Do the underlined adjectives tell *which one*, *what kind*, or *how many*?

4. The <u>lazy</u> cat was sleeping in the sun. _____

5. <u>Several</u> people saw it there on the deck. _____

Name: _____

WEEK 7
ACTIVITY 4
TOTAL /5

Correct these sentences.

1. well you certainly done a good job on youre history project
   _____

2. the feilds of golden weat in saskatchewan are quit a site to sea
   _____

Circle the adverbs.

3. here   quietly   broken   happily   fast

Write a homophone for

4. rain   _____

5. claws   _____

Name: _____

WEEK 7

ACTIVITY 5

Reference sources: atlas, almanac, dictionary, encyclopedia, thesaurus

What reference source would be best to look for information on the following:

1. information about Stanley Park _____

2. how popcorn was discovered _____

3. a synonym for "ecstatic" _____

4. The capital of the Yukon _____

5. the forecast for farmers for the coming summer _____

TOTAL /5

Name: _____

WEEK 7

Bonus Activity: Teamwork

Number these sentences in correct order to create a story.

_____ The food tasted fine but the kitchen was a disaster!

_____ My brother Dan loves to cook.

_____ One night he decided to surprise Mom by cooking dinner.

_____ Mom thanked Dan, looked at me and said, "Join me in the kitchen, Brad?"

_____ Unfortunately, he is not very good at cleaning up his mess.

_____ I'm not good at cooking, but I'm great at helping clean up!

BONUS ACTIVITY

MY CANADA

Canada's first Olympic gold medal in ice hockey was won during the 1920 Summer Games in Antwerp, Belgium. These games included a week of winter sports.

Name: _____

Correct these sentences.

1. sammy bring them nails the hammer and the screwdiver said dad
   _____

2. did you know that amelia earhart was the first women to fly a plane in newfoundlan
   _____

Write the two words that make up each contraction.

3. there's   _____   _____

4. he'd   _____   _____

Circle the example where the colon is used correctly.

5. Sincerely: Dear Uncle Max: 3:00   don:t

WEEK 8
ACTIVITY 1
TOTAL /5

Name: _____

Identify this part of a business letter.

1. Dear Mr. Gaines, CEO   _____

2. Respectfully yours   _____

Circle the word that is spelled correctly.

3. Novmber   Novemeber   November   Novemmber

Correct these sentences.

4. pioneers used oxes held together with a wooden yolk
   _____

5. there log cabins where ofen cold and damp during the long winter mouths
   _____

WEEK 8
ACTIVITY 2
TOTAL /5

28   SSR1148   ISBN: 9781771587341 © On The Mark Press

Name: _____

Common or proper noun?

WEEK 8
ACTIVITY 3
TOTAL /5

1. Chris Hadfield _____

2. spaghetti _____

Correct these sentences.

3. do you know that apple day is a poplar fundraiser for boy scouts
_____

4. canadian explorers like jacques cartier and samuel de champlain faced many dangers
_____

Is this sentence a *statement, interrogative, command* or *exclamatory*?

5. Wow! That was the best play of the game! _____

Name: _____

Correct these sentences.

WEEK 8
ACTIVITY 4
TOTAL /5

1. can you helped her solve this cerious problem with her car
_____

2. thanks penny for cleaning up that big mess they maid
_____

Divide the following word into syllables.

3. transportation _____

Write synonyms for these words.

4. liberty _____

5. hint _____

Name: _____

Combine these sentences to make one good sentence.

1. We gave Mom a box of candy. It was for Valentine's Day. The box was heart-shaped.

   _____

2. A fierce thunder storm happened yesterday. Lightning struck his barn. It burned down.

   _____

3. Watch those icy patches on the sidewalk. You might slip. You might break some bones.

   _____

4. The little kids played a board game. They played all afternoon. It was called Candyland.

   _____

5. Dad and I went camping. We went to Sand Lake Park. We slept in a tent.

   _____

WEEK 8
ACTIVITY 5
TOTAL /5

Name: _____

Bonus Activity: Are You a Happy Camper?

Create a picture that includes these objects: *tent, camp chairs, campfire, hot dogs, marshmallows, cooler,* and a *hatchet*. See if you can hide the objects so they blend into the background.

WEEK 8

MY CANADA — Apples are the most commonly grown fruit in Canada. McIntosh apples account for more than half of all the apple production.

Name: _____

WEEK 9
ACTIVITY 1
TOTAL /5

Write the word that would be last alphabetically.

1. amuse   amaze   amber   ancient   antic

2. through   though   tough   thought   touch

Correct these sentences.

3. canada's first nations people where the first people to travel buy canoe
   _____

4. early explorers didnt trust canoes sew they higher first nations guides
   _____

Circle the subject and underline the predicate in this sentence.

5. The children played hide and seek in the big back yard.

Name: _____

WEEK 9
ACTIVITY 2
TOTAL /5

Which word is not spelled correctly?

1. dollar   visitor   acter   doctor   scholar

Simile or metaphor?

2. Their new puppy is <u>as cute as a bug in a rug</u>. _____

Subject pronoun or object pronoun?

3. The boys carried it all the way home. _____

Correct these sentences.

4. them acters performed so good that the play was a success
   _____

5. whose ready for a big adventure shouted my funny uncle benny
   _____

Name: _____

Write the root word (base word) for

1. unsettled   _____

Correct these sentences.

2. prairie dogs are fury little rodents found manly in saskatchewan
_____

3. they life in prairie dog towns that is divided into smaller nieghborhoods
_____

Write the correct abbreviation for:

4. Boulevard   _____

5. Avenue   _____

WEEK 9
ACTIVITY 3
TOTAL /5

Name: _____

Correct these sentences.

1. canadas far north is filled with mountains wilderness and deep canyons
_____

2. if youre lucky youll see a iceburg as tall as a big city building
_____

Use context clues to explain the meaning of the underlined word sentence.

3. There are few motels or stores between towns so you may feel very <u>isolated</u> there.
_____

Synonyms or antonyms?

4. final, initial   _____

5. hungry, famished   _____

WEEK 9
ACTIVITY 4
TOTAL /5

32   SSR1148   ISBN: 9781771587341   © On The Mark Press

Name: _____

Write the word that best completes each sentence.

1. All week at the cottage, we _____ fish for our dinner.
   catched / caught / was catching

2. Did you know _____ both from Montreal?
   their / there / they're

3. Is your mother feeling _____ today?
   good / better / best

4. When will _____ company arrive?
   their / there / they're

5. Of all the ice cream flavours I've tried, strawberry is the _____ .
   good / better / best

WEEK **9**

ACTIVITY **5**

TOTAL **/5**

Name: _____

Bonus Activity: Odd Sound Out

Three words in each row have the same sound. **Write the word that does not belong.**

1. tube   thud   glum   jump   _____
2. kind   tile   sing   grind   _____
3. drag   clam   snag   made   _____
4. hive   find   tried   film   _____
5. hat   hatch hate   flat   _____
6. print fight cried mine   _____
7. dump   crumb spun   rule   _____
8. coat   lost   cold   bowl   _____

WEEK **9**

BONUS ACTIVITY

MY CANADA
The Halifax Gazette, first published on March 23, 1752, is Canada's oldest newspaper.

Name: _____

WEEK 10 • ACTIVITY 1 • TOTAL /5

Name the part of speech for the underlined word in each sentence.

1. We are going to miss <u>you</u> when you move. _____

2. The <u>pounding</u> rain washed out our road. _____

Correct these sentences.

3. the underground railway were a secirt network of people
   _____

4. slaves from united states escaped with help from harriet tubman
   _____

Circle the word where the apostrophe is used *incorrectly*.

5. hasn't   I'm   they've   ca'nt   she'll

Name: _____

WEEK 10 • ACTIVITY 2 • TOTAL /5

Add a prefix *and* a suffix to each word.

1. emotion _____

2. courage _____

Circle the word that comes last in alphabetical order.

3. your   yak   Yukon   yeast   youth

Correct these sentences.

4. lets meat at confederation park for a picnic with shirley and sid
   _____

5. i will brang apples juice and cookies if you like i said
   _____

Name: _____

Name the part of speech of the underlined word.

1. Our power went out <u>during</u> the bad storm. _____

Correct these sentences.

2. im gonna clean you room and put things away said the babysiter
_____

3. dont put my toys away were i cant find them wined the little boy
_____

Add a colon in the correct place.

4. 1 0 3 0

5. Take these foods

WEEK 10
ACTIVITY 3
TOTAL /5

Name: _____

Write the pronouns that would replace the underlined nouns.

(1)<u>Tom and Jerry</u> visited (2)<u>their grandmother</u> yesterday.

1. _____

2. _____

Correct these sentences.

3. we aint gots time to finish this job but well do it tomorow
_____

4. a animal got into hour garage and teared open hour garbagge
_____

Write a sentence using this pair of antonyms: rough, smooth

5. _____

WEEK 10
ACTIVITY 4
TOTAL /5

Name: _____

Decide if the underlined parts have a *capitalization error*, **a** *punctuation error*, **a** *spelling error* **or** *no mistake*.

WEEK 10

ACTIVITY 5

TOTAL /5

1. Wild turkeys are the greatest game bird in <u>north america</u>.
   _____

2. They are found <u>in southern Canada in wooded areas</u> and near farms.
   _____

3. The <u>mails</u> have sharp bony spikes on the back of each leg.
   _____

4. These spikes are called "spurs" and are <u>used for fighting?</u>
   _____

5. Do you have a hunter in your <u>family</u>. _____

Name: _____

Bonus Activity: Synonyms

WEEK 10

Solve the puzzle by filling in the correct synonym for each word clue. Write one letter in each box. Your answer must have the correct number of letters.
Clue: Write a word that means the same as:

1. stop						
2. wicked						
3. wet						
4. faint						
5. brag						
6. whole						
7. easy						
8. many						

"O Canada" was proclaimed Canada's national anthem on July 1, 1980. Before that, our national anthem was "God Save the Queen". **MY CANADA**

Name: _____

WEEK 11 — ACTIVITY 1 — TOTAL /5

Correct these sentences.

1. dont walk threw them snow angels that curtis and sharon maid
   _____

2. david juan and carla is going to cranbrook british columbia for easter
   _____

Singular possessive or plural possessive?

3. Dan's money fell into the grate on the street. _____

4. Mr. Briggs' car was stuck in the snowbank. _____

Past, present or future?

5. I have seen that movie before.   _____

Name: _____

WEEK 11 — ACTIVITY 2 — TOTAL /5

Complete the analogies.

1. Clown is to funny as ghost is to _____

2. Highway is to wide as path is to _____

Correct these sentences.

3. paul said jackie well you help me with this math problem
   _____

4. alices cat sunshine sticked it's knows into the bowl and tryed to catch the goldfish
   _____

Write the meaning of this figure of speech.

5. A farmer getting in his crops has to make hay while the sun shines.
   _____

Name: _____

WEEK 11
ACTIVITY 3
TOTAL /5

Correct these sentences.

1. canadas first prime minister was sir john a macdonald
   _____

2. in 1816 he comed to canada with his parents and lived in kingston ontario
   _____

Write the comparative and superlative forms for these adjectives.

3. lonely   _____   _____

4. busy   _____   _____

Use context to explain the meaning of the underlined word.

5. Stop <u>meddling</u> in my plans by telling me what to do.
   _____

Name: _____

WEEK 1
ACTIVITY 4
TOTAL /5

Fact or fiction?

1. Maple sap is a clear liquid that is boiled to make maple syrup. _____

2. Canada exports pineapples from its farms. _____

Correct these sentences.

3. befour starting hers day mrs jackson jogs ate kilometres down the rode
   _____

4. on aug 21 i is haveing my birthday party at parkwood beech
   _____

Simile or metaphor?

5. That boy is as stubborn as a mule. _____

Name: _____

WEEK 11

ACTIVITY 5

TOTAL /5

Reference sources: atlas, almanac, dictionary, encyclopedia, thesaurus

What reference source would be best to look for information on the following:

1. the origin of the word "moccasin" _____

2. the current population of Dartmouth, Nova Scotia _____

3. an antonym for "ridiculous" _____

4. information about the Hudson's Bay Company _____

5. the best time to plant one's garden this year _____

Name: _____

WEEK 11

BONUS ACTIVITY

Bonus Activity: Creative Compounds

Write a good sentence for each pair of compound words. Illustrate your sentence.

Compound words to use	Illustration for sentence
1. mailman, mailbox	
2. flashlight, darkness	
3. jellyfish, seashell	

Ten different types of maple trees grow in Canada. At least one kind grows naturally in every province! **MY CANADA**

Name: _____

Simile or metaphor?

WEEK **12**

1. Mac <u>is a real chicken</u> when it comes to rock climbing. _____

Correct these sentences.

ACTIVITY **1**

2. dids you read the article called canoeing in canada in canadian geographic
_____

TOTAL **/5**

3. mr connell my neighbour has teached in manitoba alberta and ontario
_____

Does the underlined adverb tell *where, when, how* or to *what extent* something happened?

4. The van veered <u>sharply</u> and spun into the ditch. _____

5. Gravel and grass flew <u>everywhere</u>. _____

Name: _____

Correct these sentences.

WEEK **12**

1. her and me was payed forteen dollars to babysit too children on saturday
_____

ACTIVITY **2**

2. the baytown animal shelter dont got no more room four rescued cats
_____

TOTAL **/5**

Write a proper noun for each common noun.

3. your favourite television show   _____

4. a good place to eat   _____

Fact or opinion?

5. Canadians are the friendliest people in the world. _____

Name: _____

Correct these sentences.

WEEK **12**

1. mr evans class planted trees in lyndhill park on earth day last year
   _____

ACTIVITY **3**

2. go teem go screemed the excited fans at the world cup game
   _____

TOTAL **/5**

Write the root word or base word for these words.

3. unfortunate   _____

4. discouraging _____

Circle the adjectives.

5. I love crispy bacon and fresh tomatoes on my toasted sandwich.

Name: _____

Correct these sentences.

WEEK **12**

1. the campers was afraid when they heared the howling of the wolfs
   _____

ACTIVITY **4**

2. mom do i really have too give the dog a bathe complaned alex
   _____

TOTAL **/5**

Present, past or future?

3. The waters in the channel froze solid last week. _____

4. The icebreaker will open a path for the ships. _____

What part of speech is the underlined word?

5. Carlos flew to <u>Brazil</u> to see his cousins. _____

Name: _____

Combine the short sentences to make one good sentence.

WEEK 12
ACTIVITY 5
TOTAL /5

1. Eli wanted to play ball. He wanted to play with his friends. He had to clean his room first.
   _____

2. Dad barbequed hamburgers. He cooked them for our lunch. We loved them.
   _____

3. My dog hurt its leg. We took her to Dr. Willows. She is our vet.
   _____

4. The cows were mooing. They were hungry. The farmer put them in the pasture.
   _____

5. Our school team won the championship. They were proud. They played their best.
   _____

Name: _____

Bonus Activity: Action Analogies

WEEK 12

Complete the analogies.

1. Run is to horse as swim is to _____

2. Sniff is to nose as wink is to _____

3. Talk is to person as quack is to _____

4. See is to eye as hear is to _____

5. Touch is to finger as smell is to _____

6. Paint is to brush as draw is to _____

When Canada became a country on July 1, 1867, there were *only four provinces*: Nova Scotia, New Brunswick, Quebec and Ontario.   **MY CANADA**

Name: _____

Underline the complete subject of this sentence.

1. Cookies, cupcakes and muffins are on sale today.

Correct these sentences.

2. dont you understand that we gots two many jobs to dew befour monday
_____

3. charlene had to sang the maple leaf forever at the seremony
_____

Underline the prepositional phrase in each sentence.

4. Make some tea in that new teapot.

5. The secretary takes messages for her boss.

WEEK
13

ACTIVITY
1

TOTAL
/5

Name: _____

Divide these words into syllables.

1. referee _____   badminton _____

Prefix or suffix?

2. correctly _____   unknown _____

Correct these sentences.

3. wood you like to play scrabble or due you wanna play monopoly
_____

4. my bother eddy eight my cookys muffen and drunk my milk
_____

Underline the predicate in this sentence.

5. My pet hamster, Angel, does funny tricks.

WEEK
13

ACTIVITY
2

TOTAL
/5

Name: _____

Is the underlined word a verb, adverb or preposition?

1. We hid under the blanket during the scary parts of the movie.
   _____

Correct these sentences.

2. when i lended you my bassball i thinked you wood retern it
   _____

3. hour uniforms gots derty from playing on that muddy feild
   _____

Does the underlined adjective tell which one, what kind, or how many?

4. Four new players joined the team. _____
5. They are all good athletes. _____

WEEK 13
ACTIVITY 3
TOTAL /5

Name: _____

Write a good sentence for this pair of homophones: straight, strait.

1. _____

Correct these sentences.

2. i readed storm fear befour i goed to sleep last nite
   _____

3. did you knitted those mitts all buy yourself asked mrs blair
   _____

Add a suffix to each word.

4. dive _____
5. marry _____

WEEK 13
ACTIVITY 4
TOTAL /5

Name: _____

Write the best word to complete each sentence.

1. That was the _____ movie I have ever seen.
   scary / scarier / scariest / more scarier

2. Everyone _____ to catch the string of the runaway kite.
   tryed / try / trying / tried

3. Harry is the _____ child in his family.
   old / oldest / older / aged

4. Was that math test the _____ you have ever taken?
   difficult / difficulter / most difficult / difficulty

5. You always finish your work _____ than your brother.
   fast / faster / fastiest / fastly

WEEK 13
ACTIVITY 5
TOTAL /5

Name: _____

Bonus Activity: Plenty of Prefixes

The prefix "*re*" means *again* or *back*. The prefix "*un*" means the *opposite of* or *not*. Complete the chart by making words with the correct prefix to match the meanings.

Meaning	Word	Meaning	Word
1. write again		5. try again	
2. not fair		6. not common	
3. not lucky		7. not healthy	
4. cover again		8. fill again	

WEEK 13

MY CANADA — The last province to become a part of Canada was Newfoundland, in 1949. How many years ago was that?

Name: _____

Correct these sentences.

1. mike broked our window it was an accident he payed to have it fixed
   _____

2. weight for the referee to blew the whistle befour you started to play
   _____

Explain the meaning of the underlined word by using context clues.

3. My baby brother is always moving and seems in <u>perpetual</u> motion.
   _____

Write the root word for these words.

4. misfortune _____

5. unbecoming _____

WEEK 14
ACTIVITY 1
TOTAL /5

Name: _____

Correct these sentences.

1. dr ashton my dentist is always very gentil with her patience
   _____

2. why is lee and stella digging wholes in there backyard
   _____

Write a synonym for.

3. anxious _____

4. difficult _____

Fact or opinion?

5. Elvis is the greatest singer of all time. _____

WEEK 14
ACTIVITY 2
TOTAL /5

Name: _____

Write the two words that make up each contraction.

WEEK **14**

1. who's _____   _____

2. they've _____   _____

ACTIVITY **3**

Correct these sentences.

3. we ask mom can we play outside in the reign
   _____

TOTAL **/5**

4. poler bare national park is on the shores of hudson bay and james bay
   _____

What part of speech is underlined in this sentence?

5. <u>Avoid</u> thin ice on that river. _____

Name: _____

Correct these sentences.

WEEK **14**

1. odessa is waring a read sweater blew pants and her knew black shoos
   _____

2. children of the wind by carl sandburg is a pome about too purple martins
   _____

ACTIVITY **4**

TOTAL **/5**

Write a common noun for these proper nouns.

3. Victoria Day _____

4. Sir John A. Macdonald _____

What is the following person's occupation?

5. Mr. Campano fixed the broken boards in our deck. _____

Name: _____

WEEK 14
ACTIVITY 5
TOTAL /5

Decide if the underlined parts have a *capitalization error*, a *punctuation error*, a *spelling error* or *no mistake*.

1. The first people that came to live in Canada long ago came from <u>asia</u>.
   _____

2. They chose <u>the Far North the Pacific coast the prairies and the Atlantic shores</u> to settle.
   _____

3. When the white men came to North America, <u>they thought they were in India</u>.
   _____

4. They called the people Indians and noticed that <u>there were many diferent groups</u>.
   _____

5. Each group had <u>their own language customs and style of clothing</u>.
   _____

Name: _____

WEEK 14
BONUS ACTIVITY

Bonus Activity: Sailors and Ships

Match a word from the Word Box with its meaning below.

1. Another name for "port" _____
2. Another name for "sailor" _____
3. It pulls other ships. _____
4. A sailor's bed _____
5. A ship's commander _____
6. It is used for steering a ship. _____
7. It carries people and cars. _____
8. A large, luxurious boat _____

9. A word for "many ships sailing together" _____
10. The back of a ship _____
11. Smoke comes from it. _____
12. It is used for rowing. _____

seafarer	harbour	bunk	yacht
oar	funnel	fleet	captain
tugboat	stern	rudder	ferry

MY CANADA
The place where Lake Ontario and Lake Erie are connected forms *Niagara Falls*.

Name: _____

Present, past or future?

1. Tony <u>dreams</u> of being an NHL hockey player some day. _____

2. He <u>will practice</u> every day if the coach asks him to do so. _____

Circle the correct abbreviation for Saturday

3. Sat   St.   Sa   Sat.   Satur.

Correct these sentences.

4. do yore friends prefer video games or board games asked ralph
_____

5. saling long ago was vary dangerous evan fore adventurous sailers
_____

WEEK 15

ACTIVITY 1

TOTAL /5

Name: _____

Write the pronoun that replaces the underlined words.

1. <u>Mom and Dad</u> are going away for the weekend. _____

Correct these sentences.

2. the caribou poler bear and beaver are canadian animals that appeer on coynes
_____

3. Dew you think it were a good idea to change won and too doller bills into coynes
_____

Synonyms, antonyms or homophones?

4. arrive, depart   _____

5. explore, investigate   _____

WEEK 15

ACTIVITY 2

TOTAL /5

SSR1148   ISBN: 9781771587341 © On The Mark Press

Name: _____

Write the plural form of:

1. tomato _____

Divide the following words into syllables.

2. influence _____

3. communication _____

Correct these sentences.

4. when you presses the buttin the elevator will starts

   _____

5. neither him nor me are going to voluntear for them jobs said ian

   _____

WEEK 15
ACTIVITY 3
TOTAL /5

Name: _____

Fact or fiction?

1. Canada is a big country with a small population. _____

2. Northern Canada is as populated as the southern parts. _____

Correct these sentences.

3. have you ever bean skiing in banff national park

   _____

4. you wood needs to obey the rules and listen to the advise of the ski patrol

   _____

Number these words in alphabetical order.

5. ____ relax   ____ release   ____ rejoice   ____ relieve   ____ reliable

WEEK 15
ACTIVITY 4
TOTAL /5

Name: _____

Write in the best word to complete each sentence.

WEEK 15
ACTIVITY 5
TOTAL /5

1. Mr. Seaman is the _____ person in our town.
   old / older / oldest

2. That mall is _____ every day of the week.
   busy / busier / busiest

3. Your drawings are the _____ .
   good / better / best

4. Put that medicine on the _____ shelf.
   high / higher / highest

5. If you do that, it will make Dad _____ .
   angry / angrier / angriest

Name: _____

WEEK 15

Bonus Activity: Prepare to Punctuate!

Read the words below. Put in the punctuation: *capitals, periods, question mark,* **and** *exclamation mark.* **Write your answers on the lines.**

1. J̶enny's birthday is in J̶anuary ·
2. may i go to the playground ___
3. the queen mary sailed across the atlantic ___
4. have you ever been on a cruise ship ___
5. we shop at loblaws and foodland ___
6. i had fun at sally's party ___
7. why were you so late, susan ___
8. how old is robert brown ___

The first design for the **loonie** showed fur-traders instead of a loon. If that design had been chosen, what do you think our one-dollar coin would be called?   **MY CANADA**

WEEK 16 — ACTIVITY 1

Name: _____

Explain the meaning of the underlined figure of speech.

1. My brother can be <u>as slow as molasses in January</u>. _____

Name the part of speech that is underlined.

2. If you help <u>others</u>, they will thank you. _____

3. Quick! Hide <u>behind</u> that tree! _____

Correct these sentences.

4. hour aunt lorraine is getting marryed on labour day weekend
_____

5. mr edwards the custodian moved them students desk in miss harts room
_____

TOTAL /5

WEEK 16 — ACTIVITY 2

Name: _____

Write a fact about the city of Ottawa.

1. _____

Does the underlined adverb tell, *how, when, where,* or *to what extent*?

2. Emily sang <u>beautifully</u> at her grandma's birthday party. _____

3. Have you seen your cousins <u>lately</u>? _____

Correct these sentences.

4. could you brang a large cold juicy watermelon to the sunday school picnic
_____

5. an old elem tree fell across our rode and blocked our weigh
_____

TOTAL /5

Name: _____

Tell the kind of sentence: *declarative, interrogative, imperative,* **or** *exclamatory.*

WEEK 16

1. What! I can't believe you have lost your money! _____

2. Go back outside and look for it right now. _____

ACTIVITY 3

Write an opinion about this topic: game shows on television

3. _____

TOTAL /5

Correct these sentences.

4. do you beleive that cars will drove theyselves in the future
   _____

5. will i read into the north or lost in the rockies for my book report
   _____

Name: _____

Correct these sentences.

WEEK 16

1. put you coat mitts hat and scarf in that there closet
   _____

ACTIVITY 4

2. what time is we due at the grand theatre for the play thumbelina
   _____

TOTAL /5

Write a common noun for each proper noun.

3. Gordie Howe _____

4. St. Lawrence _____

Circle the correct abbreviation for "post script"

5.   PS   Pst Sc   P.S.   PtSt   Ps St

Name: _____

Combine the two sentences into one good sentence.

WEEK 16
ACTIVITY 5
TOTAL /5

1. Hank is my cousin. He wants to be a cowboy. He wants to ride a horse.
   _____

2. Hank wants to live on a ranch. He wants to herd cattle. He wants to rope them too.
   _____

3. This summer he is going to Alberta. His grandfather owns a ranch. It is huge.
   _____

4. He wants to learn to ride a horse. He wants to trot and gallop. He wants to go fast.
   _____

5. He might get to round up horses. They are wild horses. It would be hard work.
   _____

Name: _____

Bonus Activity: Bundle Up! Word Search

WEEK 16
BONUS ACTIVITY

Find and circle the following words in the puzzle.

scarf   mittens
gloves   toque
coat   snow pants
sweater   boots
legwarmers
balaclava

m	s	n	o	w	p	a	n	t	s	u	j	h	o	u
s	w	t	c	e	n	b	e	r	g	b	c	k	w	h
e	e	o	i	t	b	e	l	o	n	w	a	t	n	o
o	a	n	n	a	l	b	y	r	e	r	e	s	h	q
t	t	l	e	g	w	a	r	m	e	r	s	m	o	n
w	e	t	e	r	f	l	l	l	i	i	t	o	r	t
p	r	r	i	b	s	a	s	a	o	t	h	e	g	a
b	t	e	a	r	d	c	r	k	i	d	t	e	b	t
s	t	o	o	b	r	l	a	p	i	l	o	e	i	n
g	u	t	o	o	m	a	g	r	a	t	q	e	n	f
u	l	f	g	l	o	v	e	s	f	o	u	r	y	s
o	u	p	h	e	l	a	p	i	m	s	e	b	a	c

MY CANADA

The town of Lunenburg, Nova Scotia is the birthplace of the *Bluenose*. Did you know that the name "Bluenose" is a common nickname for the people of Nova Scotia?

54   SSR1148   ISBN: 9781771587341 © On The Mark Press

Name: _____

Correct these sentences.

1. by the end of march our class will finished its study of the klondike gold rush
   _____

2. when we heard about the bad whether in quebec we canceled hour ski trip
   _____

Divide these words into syllables.

3. unpleasant _____

4. sharpener _____

Where would this probably take place?

5. Everyone screamed as the roller coaster went faster and faster. _____

WEEK **17**

ACTIVITY **1**

TOTAL /5

Name: _____

Circle the adjective. Does it tell *which one*, *what kind*, or *how many*?

1. Nature shows are filmed on location. _____

2. The first book in the series is exciting. _____

Correct these sentences.

3. jane the lifeguard waved the flagg to warn the swimmers of the strom
   _____

4. when phil send me his new email adress i will right him a massage
   _____

Circle the correct abbreviation for "Lieutenant"

5. Ltnt   Lieut.   Lten.   Lt.   Lieuten.

WEEK **17**

ACTIVITY **2**

TOTAL /5

Name: _____

WEEK 17 — ACTIVITY 3 — TOTAL /5

Tell the part of speech of the underlined word.

1. The <u>umpire</u> yelled, "You're out!" _____

2. Must you talk so <u>loudly</u>? _____

Write a good sentence for this pair of antonyms.

3. follow, lead

_____

Correct these sentences.

4. why cant aiden and art never get to hour game on time asked brad

_____

5. the wind blue so hards that hour big mapel tree losed some big branches

_____

Name: _____

WEEK 17 — ACTIVITY 4 — TOTAL /5

Fact or opinion?

1. Icebergs can be seen in the North Atlantic. _____

2. Icebergs are not a danger to ships in present times. _____

Correct these sentences.

3. the travelling theatre players is coming to our school to perform rumplestiltskin

_____

4. has you ever herd the song called this old man asked the kindergarden teacher

_____

Tell if the underlined part is the *subject* or the *predicate* of the sentence.

5. <u>Canada's first railway</u> joined the east and the west of our country.

_____

Name: _____

Explain the meaning of the underlined figures of speech.

1. My little cousin Emma <u>swims like a fish</u>.
   _____

2. I have been <u>racking my brain</u> to remember that joke.
   _____

3. What have you done? Are you <u>off your rocker</u>?
   _____

4. Eating too much junk food might make you <u>as big as a house</u>.
   _____

5. I can't get the words to that song <u>out of my head</u>.
   _____

WEEK **17**

ACTIVITY **5**

TOTAL **/5**

Name: _____

Bonus Activity: Homophone Analogies

Complete the analogies by filling in a homophone.

1. Ate is to eight as beat is to _____

2. Hear is to here as as deer is to _____

3. Cent is to sent as hair is to _____

4. Pair is to pear as sail is to _____

5. Right is to write as rode is to_____

6. Steal is to steel as meat is to _____

7. Sea is to sea as heard is to_____

8. Their is to there as stair is to_____

WEEK **17**

BONUS! ACTIVITY

MY CANADA — Canada is one of the highest water users per person in the world. Canadian household average daily use is *329 litres*.

Name: _____

Write the plural form of:

1. ox   _____

2. fox   _____

Correct these sentences.

3. canada traids lumber oil fish and wheat to countrys arownd the world
_____

4. we gots to proteckt hour naturel resources fore future genarations
_____

Write two words that rhyme with "tooth".

5. _____   _____

WEEK 18
ACTIVITY 1
TOTAL /5

Name: _____

Explain in your own words the meaning of the underlined figure of speech.

1. Your harsh words <u>cut like a knife</u>.
_____

2. That dishonest salesman sold my grandma a car that <u>was a lemon</u>.
_____

Correct these sentences.

3. mom likes to sing lullabys like rock a bye baby to my baby sister pam
_____

4. because my sister pauline and me was born on the same day we have won big party
_____

Circle the word with the most syllables.

5. Thanksgiving   orchestra   communication   arrangement

WEEK 18
ACTIVITY 2
TOTAL /5

Name: _____

Correct these sentences.

1. dr and mr briggs is excited about there vaction plans to go to vancover
   _____

2. bill dont need no help with her homework assignmint
   _____

Tell whether the underlined verb is present, past or future.

3. He <u>has travelled</u> many miles to see you.   _____

4. Please be on time when you <u>meet</u> tomorrow.   _____

Singular or plural?

5. people   _____

WEEK 18
ACTIVITY 3
TOTAL /5

Name: _____

Declarative, interrogative, imperative, or exclamatory?

1. What is the worst thing that might happen on this hike?   _____

Correct these sentences.

2. was the acters nervous befour the play beginned
   _____

3. milly picked a apple from hour tree she took a big bit
   _____

Where would these events likely take place?

4. He baited his hook and dropped the line into the water.
   _____

5. The cashier scanned each item and packed them carefully into a bag.
   _____

WEEK 18
ACTIVITY 4
TOTAL /5

Name: _____

Reference sources: atlas, almanac, dictionary, encyclopedia, thesaurus

What reference source would be best to look for information on the following:

1. The pronunciation of the word " aurora" _____
2. a picture of the world's largest Easter egg _____
3. information on Martin Frobisher _____
4. an synonym for the word "hungry" _____
5. the latitude and longitude for Toronto _____

WEEK 18
ACTIVITY 5
TOTAL /5

Name: _____

Bonus Activity: Sounds Like...

Choose a words from the box that describes how each of these things sound.

| crow squeak cluck bark chirp roar jangle slam neigh quack buzz honk |

1. Horses _____
2. Ducks _____
3. Hens _____
4. Lions _____
5. Bees _____
6. Mice _____
7. Roosters _____
8. Doors _____
9. Chains _____
10. Sparrows _____
11. Dogs _____
12. Horns _____

WEEK 18

MY CANDA *The famous Vachon snack cake, Jos Louis, was named after two of the owners' sons: Joseph and Louis.*

Name: _____

WEEK 19 — ACTIVITY 1 — TOTAL /5

Correct these sentences.

1. the mother wolfe gots ate fury chubby pups in her letter
   _____

2. all poeple animals and plants needs fresh cleen water to life
   _____

Write in the best word to complete this sentence.

3. _____ you finished eating your lunch yet?
   Are not / Ain't / Aren't / Arent

Give a synonym for each word.

4. hard   _____   _____

5. frosty   _____   _____

Name: _____

WEEK 19 — ACTIVITY 2 — TOTAL /5

Circle the word that does not belong in this group.

1. loon   puffin   robin   ostrich   sparrow   blue jay

Correct these sentences.

2. look out him called the tree branch is falling neer you
   _____

3. marty seed a animal dug into the garbage bag last knight
   _____

Present, past or *future*?

4. Todd learned how to skate when he was five years old.   _____

5. I will meet you at the movies.   _____

Name: _____

Circle the correct abbreviation for "Professor".

1. Proff.   Pro   Prof.   Pros   Profs.

Is the underlined part the subject or the predicate of the sentence?

2. <u>Delicious strawberries</u> grew in big bunches on the plants. _____

3. The mother bird <u>protected the eggs in her nest</u>. _____

Correct these sentences.

4. luke eated most of hims hot dog he left sum of the bun

   _____

5. do you has the fone number for chubby chicken take-out on main street

   _____

WEEK 19
ACTIVITY 3
TOTAL /5

Name: _____

Divide these words into syllables.

1. intersection   _____

2. proportion   _____

Write the pronoun that would replace the underlined words.

3. That baseball bat belongs to <u>Matt and Mike</u>. _____

Correct these sentences.

4. after you done your chores you can play outside said mom

   _____

5. i my try out for the socer team or i my join track and feild

   _____

WEEK 19
ACTIVITY 4
TOTAL /5

Name: _____

WEEK 19
ACTIVITY 5
TOTAL /5

Combine these sentences to make one good sentence.

1. The little children sang in the play. They danced too. The parents watched them.
   _____

2. Grandpa has a big garden. He grows corn. He grows tomatoes. He grows beans.
   _____

3. I have an aunt named Mel. She lives in New Brunswick. She has lived there for 10 years.
   _____

4. There was a big storm last night. It was a snow storm. Today will be a snow day for us.
   _____

5. Our school had a talent contest. Fifteen people entered. Sarah won with her magic act.
   _____

Name: _____

WEEK 19
BONUS ACTIVITY

Bonus Activity: Reading Skills

Read this paragraph. Circle the letter of the correct answer for each sentence.

Anna thought her best birthday present was her model airplane. She read all the instructions and then carefully put the pieces together. When the plane was finished, she painted it pink and green. How proud she was to have built it all by herself!

1. The main idea of the paragraph is:
   a) Anna painted her plane.   b) Anna enjoyed building her plane.
   c) Anna received birthday presents.

2. Anna painted her plane:
   a) brown and green   b) yellow and green   c) pink and green.

3. The best title for this paragraph is:
   a) The Best Birthday Present   b) Anna's Airplane   c) Building is Fun

MY CANADA
The Great Bear rain forest in British Columbia has trees that reach 95 metres. Sadly, its survival is more threatened than the tropical rain forests.

Name: _____

Circle the correct abbreviation for "Junior"

1. Jr   Jun   Jr.   Jun.   Jn

Write the meaning of the underlined figures of speech.

2. My uncle has <u>a green thumb</u>. _____

3. Sometimes she acts <u>batty</u>. _____

Correct these sentences.

4. is this what you was looking four asked the saleslady
   _____

5. my freinds threw me a suprise birthday party last saturday nite
   _____

WEEK 20
ACTIVITY 1
TOTAL /5

Name: _____

Correct these sentences.

1. dont touch that read hot pane on the stove warned allan
   _____

2. ari likes to reads folk tails about talking animals and unusual places
   _____

Divide each word into syllables.

3. obligation _____

4. nevertheless _____

Circle the cause and underline the effect.

5. I need to get the flu shot because I get sick easily.

WEEK 20
ACTIVITY 2
TOTAL /5

Name: _____

Write the root word for this word.

1. undetected   _____

Correct these sentences.

2. devin said i hope he choose me to bee on his teem
   _____

3. sometimes he feel like going outside and sometimes he dont
   _____

Underline all the adverbs in these sentences.

4. Aim accurately, shoot straight and you may hit the target.

5. The wolf huffed loudly, puffed strongly and cheered gleefully when the house fell down.

WEEK 20
ACTIVITY 3
TOTAL /5

Name: _____

Write three words that rhyme with

1. ghost   _____

2. cone   _____

Correct these sentences.

3. were leaving for calgary tonite on air canadas 6 oclock flight
   _____

4. my ant and uncle will meat us at the airport at 9 oclock sharpe
   _____

Circle the word that does not belong.

5. kayak   canoe   sea-doo   wagon   surfboard

WEEK 20
ACTIVITY 4
TOTAL /5

Name: _____

Write in the best word to complete each sentence.

1. My sister Esther looked so beautiful as she walked down the _____.
   isle / aisle / I'll

2. Her pet rabbit _____ a whole head of lettuce yesterday.
   eight / eats / ate

3. How much _____ is there in cutting grass in your neighbourhood?
   profit / prophet / product

4. The _____ of that perfume is very strong.
   sent / cent / scent

5. How many _____ does your dentist have?
   patience / patients / patterns

WEEK 20
ACTIVITY 5
TOTAL /5

Name: _____

Bonus Activity: It's a Date!

When we write the date we use:
- a capital letter for the month
- numerals for the numbers
- a comma before the year

Write the following dates.

1. the last day of this year _____

2. the date for the next Christmas Day _____

3. next Sunday's date _____

4. the date you were born _____

5. today's date _____

6. a date that is important to you _____ This date is _____

WEEK 20
BONUS ACTIVITY

MY CANADA — Canada's highest mountain peak is Mount Logan, Yukon at 5959 metres. It is part of the St. Elias Mountains.

Name: _____

WEEK 21
ACTIVITY 1
TOTAL /5

Explain in your own words the meaning of the underlined figures of speech.

1. You had better <u>button your lip</u> before you get into trouble.
   _____

2. She <u>bends over backwards</u> to do her best work.
   _____

Correct these sentences.

3. dont forgot to feed an water the dog befour you go to sckool reminded dad
   _____

4. The vue from the mountin dont look like nothing ive ever seen before
   _____

Write the possessive noun:

5. the new boots belong to Jeremy _____

Name: _____

WEEK 21
ACTIVITY 2
TOTAL /5

Correct these sentences.

1. frogs snakes and water bugs life in hour pound in the backyard
   _____

2. we always goes to the beech wen the whether is sew hot
   _____

Do these words have a *prefix* or a *suffix*?

3. agreeable _____

4. unwell _____

Tell if the pair of words are *synonyms*, *antonyms*, or *homophones*?

5. unique, unusual _____

Name: _____

WEEK 21

ACTIVITY 3

TOTAL /5

Where would this event probably be happening?

1. "All passengers bound for Fort McMurray may board now."
   _____

Correct these sentences.

2. seth are spending august at hims grandparents cottage in the muskokas
   _____

3. well you help us built an snow fort in bridwell park on sunday
   _____

Are the underlined words a *subject pronoun* or a *possessive pronoun*?

4. Ollie loves <u>his</u> new puppy, Patches. _____

5. <u>They</u> wanted to share their good fortune with their family. _____

Name: _____

WEEK 21

ACTIVITY 4

TOTAL /5

Correct these sentences.

1. them storys that our camp counceller telled was really scary
   _____

2. has you ever went water-skiing on lake winnipeg
   _____

Write the comparative and superlative forms of these adjectives.

3. lucky   _____

4. crazy   _____

Write three words that rhyme with "house".

5. house   _____

Name: _____

Decide if the underlined parts have a *capitalization error*, a *punctuation error*, a *spelling error* or *no mistake*.

WEEK 21
ACTIVITY 5
TOTAL /5

1. Dad decided my brother, <u>robert</u>, and I should go ice fishing. _____

2. We bundled up in <u>warm suits mitts toques and boots.</u> _____

3. Soon we were off <u>with all our gear and some lunch Mom had made.</u> _____

4. We loaded <u>our things onto a slay</u> and headed out onto the lake. _____

5. We met our uncle <u>at his small fishing shack on crow lake.</u> _____

Name: _____

Bonus Activity: Know Your Fruits and Veggies!

WEEK 21

Read the sentence clues. Use a word from the Word Box that could fit in the blank.

> raisin   lettuce   tomato   banana   cucumber   apple
> radish   corner   potato   lemon   watermelon   pumpkin

1. a red fruit for salads _____
2. can be used to make pie _____
3. long yellow fruit _____
4. red vegetable with a hot taste _____
5. can be used to make pickles _____
6. can be yellow, green or red _____
7. ears of _____
8. has sour juice _____
9. grows under the ground _____
10. leaf used in salad _____
11. very large fruit _____
12. sweet, dried grape _____

MY CANADA   *The Butterfly Conservatory in Cambridge, Ontario displays one of Canada's largest insect collections. Visitors can observe over 2000 free-flying butterflies.*

Name: _____

Underline the prepositions in these sentences.

1. He found his slipper under the couch.

2. We threw the ball high into the air.

Write a word that belongs in this group.

3. mauve   scarlet   aqua   violet   _____

Correct these sentences.

4. has you rode on a paddle boat on kings lake yet
   _____

5. linda shouted look a double reinbow ive never seed won before
   _____

WEEK 22
ACTIVITY 1
TOTAL /5

Name: _____

Write five words that rhyme with "care".

1. _____

Write the pronoun for the underlined words.

2. Vicki and Josh are in Grade 5.   _____

3. Are you going tobogganing with Doug?   _____

Correct these sentences.

4. michelle maggie and lucy is commin to my hose for sunday dinner
   _____

5. the hole teem is gonna go to pizza palace after the game said coach wills
   _____

WEEK 22
ACTIVITY 2
TOTAL /5

Name: _____

Write a common noun for each proper noun.

1. Albertosaurus _____

2. Labour Day _____

Circle the words that have four syllables.

3. semicircle   frequently   bicycle   motorcycle   hemisphere

Correct these sentences.

4. i can sea that well have them little kids rebuilt there snowman
   _____

5. me and jim was excited about running in the terry fox marathon of hope
   _____

WEEK 22
ACTIVITY 3
TOTAL /5

Name: _____

Tell what this person's job would be.

1. They protect animals and fish from the illegal actions of hunters and fishermen.
   _____

Correct these sentences.

2. there goalie breaked his ankel he cant play hockey with the teem
   _____

3. lets have a adventure in that there glomy cave said andy
   _____

Use context clues to explain the meaning of the underlined words.

4. If you stay until the end of the play, you will see the <u>grand finale</u>.
   _____

5. That picture looks odd because the frame is an <u>irregular</u> shape.
   _____

WEEK 22
ACTIVITY 4
TOTAL /5

Name: _____

Explain in your own words the meaning of the underlined figures of speech.

WEEK 22

ACTIVITY 5

1. Climbing that mountain would <u>be a tall order</u> for me.
   _____

2. Everyone was <u>as quiet as a mouse</u> in the library.
   _____

TOTAL /5

3. <u>Don't count your chickens before they hatch</u> is a good saying to remember.
   _____

4. My new skates will cost <u>an arm and a leg</u>.
   _____

5. All that racket has given me a <u>splitting headache</u>.
   _____

Name: _____

Bonus Activity: Colourful Parts of Speech.

WEEK 22

BONUS ACTIVITY

Read the words in the boxes. Then colour the square using this code.

Nouns: red   Adjectives: green   Verbs: blue   Adverbs: orange

mouse	loudly	grey	rapidly	furiously	dash
spray	busy	mole	scurry	rabbit	timid
softly	quickly	sassy	lively	secretly	dig
skunk	bold	chipmunk	squeak	hide	squirrel

MY CANADA

Baffin Island, Nunavut, is the largest island in Canada and fifth largest in the world. It is estimated that there are about 10,000 glaciers in Baffin Island.

Name: _____

Correct these sentences.

1. they herd thunder seen lighting and felt rein during the strom

   _____

2. what happened here this hole house is won big mess

   _____

Use context clues to explain the meaning of the underlined word.

3. She has always loved castles so they have built a <u>turret</u> on one end of their house.

   _____

Add one more word to each group.

4. mathematics   science   history   art   _____

5. New Year's Day   Valentine's Day   Easter   St. Patrick's Day   _____

WEEK 23

ACTIVITY 1

TOTAL /5

Name: _____

Correct these sentences.

1. wow what a grate looking sports care exclaimed hal

   _____

2. speek softly we dont went nobody to here hour secret

   _____

Present, past or *future*?

3. On my next birthday I am going to Canada's Wonderland.   _____

4. I went last year with my cousins.   _____

Identify this part of a friendly letter.

5. Let's plan to go to the beach a week from Saturday.   _____

WEEK 23

ACTIVITY 2

TOTAL /5

Name: _____

Correct these sentences.

1. pete yelled too warn kevin but it were to late
   _____

2. hour teem will play at 2 oclock sharpe at cook's arena
   _____

Tell if these words are *synonyms* or *antonyms*.

3. dim, gloomy   _____

Divide the following words into syllables.

4. dilapidated   _____

5. innocent   _____

WEEK **23**
ACTIVITY **3**
TOTAL /5

Name: _____

In which part of a business letter would the following be found?

1. Dear Mr. Hermann: _____

Write the singular form of these words.

2. knives   _____

3. babies   _____

Correct these sentences.

4. stopping by woods on a snowy evening by robert frost is a well none pome
   _____

5. the family that lived next dore goed to another city to life
   _____

WEEK **23**
ACTIVITY **4**
TOTAL /5

Name: _____

Reference sources: atlas, almanac, dictionary, encyclopedia, thesaurus

WEEK 23

ACTIVITY 5

TOTAL /5

What reference source would be best to look for information on the following:

1. The distance from Saskatoon to Winnipeg _____

2. The average temperature expected in May in Manitoba _____

3. what direction you would travel to reach Ellesmere Island _____

4. what a porcupine eats _____

5. a synonym for the word "complex" _____

Name: _____

Bonus Activity: Wild Weather!

WEEK 23

BONUS ACTIVITY

Canada has all kinds of weather. **Write the correct word that matches the clue.**

| rain   drizzle   gale   frost   lightning   smog   fog   blizzard   thunder   hail |

1. frozen dew _____
2. smoke and fog _____
3. electricity in the sky _____
4. water from clouds _____
5. noise in the sky _____
6. thick mist _____
7. frozen rain _____
8. violent snowstorm _____
9. very strong wind _____
10. a light rain _____

MY CANADA

The Toronto Zoo greets about 1.5 million visitors each year. The estimated cost to feed all of the zoo's creatures is $750,000.

WEEK 24 — ACTIVITY 1

Name: _____

Use context to explain the meaning of the underlined word in this sentence.

1. Use your <u>serviette</u> to wipe off your hands so your clothes stay clean.
   _____

Correct these sentences.

2. after diggin four too ours them men were covered with dert
   _____

3. did youre sister promise to arrive by 7 oclock for the meating
   _____

Complete the analogies.

4. a boulder is heavy, a pebble is _____

5. a shout is loud, a whisper is _____

TOTAL /5

WEEK 24 — ACTIVITY 2

Name: _____

Fact or opinion?

1. Eating vegetables can help you become a healthier person. _____

2. All green vegetables should be eaten raw. _____

Correct these sentences.

3. both boys bikes were read with blew raceing strips
   _____

4. we has saled on uncle freds saleboat at least ate times
   _____

Tell if this sentence is *declarative, interrogative, exclamatory* or *imperative*.

5. Get this mess cleaned up immediately. _____

TOTAL /5

Name: _____

WEEK 24
ACTIVITY 3
TOTAL /5

Synonym or *antonym*?

1. group, individual _____

Correct these sentences.

2. codys friends was afraid of the dark his mom gived them a flashlite
   _____

3. them greedy boys drinked all the cold milk we done had
   _____

Write the pronoun that would replace the underlined noun.

4. <u>My sister</u> won first place in public speaking. _____

5. <u>Her prize</u> was $25 so she was very happy. _____

Name: _____

WEEK 24
ACTIVITY 4
TOTAL /5

Correct these sentences.

1. has you ever red the kids almanac asked jake
   _____

2. we all singed happy birthday before roxanne cut the cake
   _____

Common or *proper noun*?

3. skateboard _____

4. Burger King _____

Tell if the underlined word is a *noun*, *verb* or *adjective*.

5. Run <u>fast</u> and they won't catch you. _____

Name: _____

Combine these sentences to make one good sentence.

WEEK 24
ACTIVITY 5
TOTAL /5

1. One hot day, we bought ice cream cones. We sat on the park bench. We ate our cones.
   _____

2. Our teacher read us three poems. They were funny poems. She read them to us today.
   _____

3. The fans watched the ball game. They cheered for the home team. The home team won.
   _____

4. The cookie jar is empty now. It had six cookies left. My brother ate six cookies.
   _____

5. We walked along the crowded street. We saw puppies. We looked in the shop windows.
   _____

Name: _____

Bonus Activity: The Great Canadian Scramble

WEEK 24
BONUS ACTIVITY

Unscramble these letters to spell the names of great Canadian landmarks.

1. CORYK   NAITSOUNM   _____

2. RAGAIAN   LLFAS   _____

3. OCEV   GGS'YPE   _____

4. DNALTRAH   DEREVOC   EGDIRB   _____

5. CORK   RECEP   _____

Alert, a Canadian Forces Station, on Ellesmere Island, is the world's most northern permanently inhabited settlement.

MY CANADA

Name: _____

Correct these sentences.

1. are them sallys favourite red shoos asked daisy
   _____

2. callie done the cookin and cleanin to suprise her mother
   _____

Underline the adverbs in each sentence.

3. We are going swimming tomorrow.

4. Stand straight and I will measure you.

Write the two words used to make this contraction.

5. I'd _____

WEEK **25**
ACTIVITY **1**
TOTAL **/5**

Name: _____

Correct these sentences.

1. you arent the boss of me yelled the knotty little boy
   _____

2. jonah leap on hims snow board and saled down the mountin
   _____

Past, present or *future*?

3. The secret will soon be out. _____

How many syllables in each word?

4. Medicine Hat _____

5. Portage la Prairie _____

WEEK **25**
ACTIVITY **2**
TOTAL **/5**

Name: _____

WEEK 25 — ACTIVITY 3 — TOTAL /5

Simile or metaphor?

1. Hayden can run like the wind. _____

2. The wind moaned and groaned throughout the night. _____

Correct these sentences.

3. spots tale wagged as i given him the babys leftovers
   _____

4. when well the technician mr carrell fix hour computer
   _____

Number these words in alphabetical order.

5. ___ morsel   ___ mortal   ___ moral   ___ more   ___ morning

---

Name: _____

WEEK 25 — ACTIVITY 4 — TOTAL /5

Correct these sentences.

1. what dew you likes on your burger and hot dog asked max
   _____

2. them terrible winds blue a umbrella and chare write of hour deck
   _____

Add a prefix and a suffix to this word.

3. appear   _____

Fact or fantasy?

4. The dragon's fiery breath scorched all the land in the kingdom. _____

5. Prince Harry has visited Canada. _____

Name: _____

Write in the best word to complete each sentence.

1. How many baby _____ were born to your pet rabbit?
   bunnys / bunnies' / bunnies / bunny's

2. Please give a cup of hot chocolate to _____.
   he / they / him / I

3. _____ going hiking with you?
   Whose / Who's / Who / Whom

4. My brother _____ married in 2000.
   was / were / been / did

5. When _____ you need a ride to school?
   does / do / was / is

WEEK 25
ACTIVITY 5
TOTAL /5

Name: _____

Bonus Activity: Reading Skills

Read the paragraph. Read the sentences. Circle T if the sentence is *true* and F if it is *false*.

You ever looked out into your flower garden and seen hummingbirds? They come in many sizes. Some grow to fifteen centimetres long. Others are as small as two centimetres. That is no longer than a bee! These birds get their name from the humming sound made by their wings. A hummingbird can stay in one place in the air. This is called hovering. By flapping its wings very fast, it can remain as if hanging by a string.

1. T F Hummingbirds can grow up to eighteen centimetres long.
2. T F Hummingbirds get their name from the sound made by their wings.
3. T F Hovering means "staying in one place in the air."
4. T F A hummingbird flies in circles to remain in the air.

WEEK 25

Canada's only *potato museum* opened in 1993 in O'Leary, P.E.I. It contains the world's largest collection of artifacts. **MY CANADA**

Name: _____

WEEK 26

ACTIVITY 1

TOTAL /5

Explain these idioms.

1. She has a heart of gold. _____

2. He had a frog in his throat. _____

Correct these sentences.

3. prof lewis orderd them special specimans of exotic insects didnt he
   _____

4. the boys was hungry tried and derty after helping use build the treehouse
   _____

Write the preposition in this sentence.

5. We went skating on the Rideau Canal. _____

Name: _____

WEEK 26

ACTIVITY 2

TOTAL /5

Complete the analogies.

1. Bird is to fly as frog is to _____

2. Laugh is to happy as cry is to _____

Write the two words that make up this contraction.

3. who'll _____

Correct these sentences.

4. did ewe no in february snow fell everyday in the maritimes
   _____

5. the athens figure skating club were the best in the area dont you agree
   _____

Name: _____

Singular possessive or plural possessive?

1. the babies' toys   _____

2. Jackson's skateboard   _____

Correct these sentences.

3. how many peaces of punkin pie did tony ate asked julie
   _____

4. them boys is gonna bee in trouble for walking on ann's floor with them dirty boots
   _____

Write the *past* and the *future tense* for the following verb.

5. satisfy   _____   _____

WEEK 26
ACTIVITY 3
TOTAL /5

Name: _____

Correct these sentences.

1. why doesnt people made homemade ice creem today inquired jessica
   _____

2. them kids all choosed junior scrabble as there favorite bored game to play
   _____

Where would you hear the following?

3. "You must be five feet tall to go on this ride." _____

4. "This shot will help to keep you healthy this winter." _____

Write the root word for this word.

5. disappointment   _____

WEEK 26
ACTIVITY 4
TOTAL /5

Name: _____

Decide if the underlined parts have a *capitalization error*, a *punctuation error*, a *spelling error* or *no mistake*.

WEEK **26**

ACTIVITY **5**

TOTAL **/5**

1. <u>sugaring</u> off is a fun activity in the sugar bush.
   _____

2. People gather to boil down sap <u>to make maple suger</u> and candy.
   _____

3. A favourite treat is taffy made <u>when hot thick syrup is poured</u> on snow.
   _____

4. The syrup hardens quickly <u>so you will need to be fast with your fork</u>.
   _____

5. <u>Watch out Don't burn yourself</u> trying to take a bite.
   _____

Name: _____

Bonus Activity: Using a Thesaurus

WEEK **26**

A *thesaurus* is a reference source that gives us **synonyms** and **antonyms** for words. **Complete the chart by writing one synonym and one antonym for each word.** Use a thesaurus if you need help.

Word	Synonym	Antonym
1. dark		
2. graceful		
3. luck		
4. partner		
5. stay		

MY CANADA — The Trans-Canada Highway is the world's longest national road. Its construction began in 1950.

Name: _____

Correct these sentences.

WEEK **27**

ACTIVITY **1**

1. they has gone shopping four soccer sox shorts cleets and headbands
   _____

2. there favorite story is i want that dog by jean little
   _____

TOTAL **/5**

Is the underlined part the *subject* or the *predicate* of the sentence?

3. Herbie <u>should be cleaning</u> his room.   _____

4. <u>The entire team</u> deserves credit for winning the game. _____

Write an opinion about this topic: settling Canada's north

5. _____

Name: _____

Declarative, interrogative, imperative, or exclamatory?

WEEK **27**

ACTIVITY **2**

1. What a great adventure!   _____

2. Pick up those Lego blocks.   _____

Write the number of syllables in this word.

TOTAL **/5**

3. atmosphere   _____

Correct these sentences.

4. they is moved to a new apartmant at 666 south street in calgary
   _____

5. after the seads sprouted into littel plants they growed quickly in one weak
   _____

Name: _____

Use context clues to explain the meaning of the underlined words.

1. Builders need to make certain the <u>scaffold</u> is secure before they start the roof.
   _____

2. Mark these sentences in your notes as I will <u>emphasize</u> them on the test.
   _____

Correct these sentences.

3. you mustnt leaf the house wile yore parents is gone shopping
   _____

4. uncle fred bot us fries pogos tacos and wraps for bens party
   _____

Number these words in alphabetical order.

5. ___crocodile   ___croquet   ___crossbow   ___crocus   ___crouch

WEEK 27
ACTIVITY 3
TOTAL /5

Name: _____

Write four words that rhyme with "close"

1. _____

Correct these sentences.

2. is we supposed to read the chapter on henry hudson or on martin frobisher
   _____

3. the explorers who tryed to find the northwest passage was very brave
   _____

Does the underlined adjective tell *which one, what kind* or *how many*?

4. The <u>orange</u> kitten looks like Garfield. _____

5. The <u>blinding</u> snowstorm made driving dangerous. _____

WEEK 27
ACTIVITY 4
TOTAL /5

86   SSR1148   ISBN: 9781771587341   © On The Mark Press

Name: _____

Explain the meaning of the underlined phrases.

WEEK **27**

ACTIVITY **5**

TOTAL /5

1. This story came <u>right from the horse's mouth</u>. It must be true.
   _____

2. Ford knows a lot of words. He is <u>a walking dictionary</u>.
   _____

3. <u>Time stood still</u> as we waited for the big announcement.
   _____

4. "Why are you always <u>bugging me</u>?" I asked my brother.
   _____

5. Johnny was smiling from <u>ear to ear</u> as he received the trophy.
   _____

Name: _____

Bonus Activity: Maple Goodness

WEEK **27**

Find and circle the following words in the puzzle.

delicious	pipelines
spigots	boil
syrup	gather
maple	tractor
buckets	sweet
sap	

d	e	l	i	c	i	o	u	s	l	s	n
o	t	w	t	e	v	i	a	y	i	p	t
u	r	o	s	o	g	p	o	r	o	i	e
g	a	t	h	e	r	a	m	u	b	g	e
l	c	a	m	a	p	l	e	p	w	o	w
l	t	i	p	p	b	u	c	k	e	t	s
c	o	e	l	o	e	b	r	c	r	s	w
s	r	p	i	p	e	l	i	n	e	s	e

MY CANADA

Over 300 dinosaur skeletons have been excavated from the Drumheller Badlands in Alberta. About 35 species used to roam where Dinosaur Provincial Park now stands.

Name: _____

Divide these words into syllables.

1. Bombardier _____

2. snowmobile _____

Correct these sentences.

3. i cant never decide which i like best -- sking ore toboganing
   _____

4. because i braked my leg i missed too birthday partys
   _____

Write the present tense of the verb in this sentence.

5. We forget what we needed to do. _____

WEEK 28
ACTIVITY 1
TOTAL /5

Name: _____

Where would the following probably take place?

1. The professor shook George's hand and handed him his diploma.
   _____

Correct these sentences.

2. derek will need a knew break on hims bike before hell be able to rase
   _____

3. them little kids got wet frum wadding in them puddles and splashing each another.
   _____

Fact or *fiction*?

4. Paul Bunyan made the 1000 Islands with shovelfuls of dirt. _____

5. You can cruise the 1000 islands on a tour boat. _____

WEEK 28
ACTIVITY 2
TOTAL /5

Name: _____

Do these adverbs tell *how*, *where*, or to *what extent* something happens?

1. That little boy talks <u>nonstop</u>. _____

2. Play that noisy game <u>outside</u>, please. _____

Underline the synonyms in the following sentence.

3. Does your elderly uncle still drive that old John Deere tractor?

Correct these sentences.

4. did you see lost mines of the north on television last knight
   _____

5. dad blue a tyre when he hit a large potwhole in the rode on tuesday
   _____

WEEK 28
ACTIVITY 3
TOTAL /5

Name: _____

Punctuate this date correctly.

1. Mon Aug 21 2007 _____

Correct these sentences.

2. we are leaving for the canadian museum of civilization at 8 oclock sharp tomorow
   _____

3. events at the calgary stampede include bull riding roping barrel racing and bronc riding
   _____

Where would the following probably take place?

4. The big jet taxied out onto the runway and started to pick up speed.
   _____

5. The workers checked each new van as it came off the assembly line.
   _____

WEEK 28
ACTIVITY 4
TOTAL /5

Name: _____

Reference sources: atlas, almanac, dictionary, encyclopedia, thesaurus

What reference source would be best to look for information on the following:

1. information about the Halifax Explosion   _____

2. where beluga whales live   _____

3. a synonym for "glisten"   _____

4. The average temperature of Gander, NFL. in June   _____

5. the location of Prince Albert National Park   _____

WEEK 28

ACTIVITY 5

TOTAL /5

Name: _____

Bonus Activity: Just for Fun: Anagrams

Rearrange the letters in the given word to make a new word. Then tell the meaning of the new word. The first one is done for you.

Make this word	Into a new word	Meaning of new word
1. reap	pear	a yellow or green fruit
2. low	_____	_____
3. leak	_____	_____
4. was	_____	_____
5. slap	_____	_____
6. tool	_____	_____

WEEK 28

The last spike of Canada's transcontinental railroad was driven in Craigellachie, a small British Columbia settlement, in 1885.

MY CANADA

Name: _____

Correct these sentences.

1. we climed to the top of rock dunder what a amazing view

   _____

2. if gabe striked out this here time we will loose the finale game

   _____

WEEK 29

ACTIVITY 1

TOTAL /5

Singular or *plural* **noun?**

3. sheep   _____

4. knives   _____

Write three words that rhyme with "please".

5. _____

Name: _____

Correct these sentences.

1. did you no that alexander graham bell was co – inventor of the first hydrofoil

   _____

2. he also maid the first won-way long-distance telephone call between too towns in ontario

   _____

WEEK 29

ACTIVITY 2

TOTAL /5

Use context clues to explain the meaning of the underlined words.

3. Who will be our travelling <u>companion</u> when you go to England?

   _____

4. Judy <u>hobbled</u> around on her sprained ankle for two weeks.

   _____

Declarative, exclamatory, interrogative, **or** *imperative*?

5. Our school is the best!   _____

Name: _____

Correct these sentences.

1. you gotta work real hard to beet my friend jerry
   _____

2. mrs hart the school secretary is very polit to all visiters
   _____

Common or *proper noun*?

3. bald eagle   _____

4. Sparky the Fire Dog   _____

Circle the adjectives in this sentence.

5. Who is that little boy wearing the brown furry coat?

WEEK
29

ACTIVITY
3

TOTAL
/5

Name: _____

Write the root or base word for these words.

1. population   _____

2. disregarding   _____

Correct these sentences.

3. there mom is lookin fore a knew job at bayside library in fort william
   _____

4. wen i were a little girl we live in brandon manitoba
   _____

Divide this word into syllables.

5. temperature   _____

WEEK
29

ACTIVITY
4

TOTAL
/5

Name: _____

Write in the best word to complete each sentence.

1. He _____ that tiny fish back into the lake.
   through / threw / throwed

2. Mike was _____ the marshmallows for our campfire treat.
   bring / brought / bringing

3. Someone _____ to collect some wood for our campfire.
   needing / need / needs

4. Remember to invite Cameron and _____ cousin, Carter.
   hims / him / his

5. We might stay for two _____ if our parents agree.
   nights / nites / knights

WEEK 29
ACTIVITY 5
TOTAL /5

Name: _____

Bonus Activity: General Store Goods Unscramble

Long ago there was one main store in town—the General Store.
Unscramble these words to correctly spell the names of things you could buy there.

1. oodf _____
2. lcothnig _____
3. nugs _____
4. oslot _____
5. srpeapewns _____
6. soty _____
7. numaitimon _____
8. libnugid eritamals _____

WEEK 29

MY CANADA
The Norlund Chapel, one of the smallest churches in the world, is located in Emo, Ontario. It is 11 metres high and can only hold eight people at one time.

Name: _____

Write a word that belongs in this group.

1. lake   bay   stream   pond   _____

Correct these sentences.

2. each saturday at 10:00 my little sister watches strawberry shortcake on television
   _____

3. i am reading won chapter of holes every knight before i go to sleep
   _____

Circle the word that is spelled correctly.

4. interier   intirior   interyor   enterior   interior

5. camara   camira   camera   kamera   kemara

WEEK 30
ACTIVITY 1
TOTAL /5

Name: _____

Opinion or fact?

1. Gary will be picked for the team because he is such a good player. _____

Correct these sentences.

2. hour grandparents taked both familys to the golden dragon to selebrate
   _____

3. after working for ate ours caleb and ryan finish the rale fence
   _____

What part of speech is the underlined word: *noun, verb, adjective, adverb*?

4. The <u>ancient</u> statue toppled over.   _____

5. The <u>demolition</u> on the old building has begun.   _____

WEEK 30
ACTIVITY 2
TOTAL /5

Name: _____

Correct these sentences.

1. reva bought her favorite book red fern at book traders on king street
   _____

2. paula may i stay with you in yore cabin at kid camp this summer
   _____

Write the past and future tense of "go".

3. _____

Number these words in alphabetical order.

4. ____ elegant ____ elbow ____ elf ____ elastic ____ elephant

5. ____ post ____ postal ____ postage ____ post card ____ post office

WEEK **30**
ACTIVITY **3**
TOTAL **/5**

Name: _____

Correct these sentences.

1. the sircus are in town yelled tammy i see the monkeys in that there truck
   _____

2. every day people hurry too work too school two shop and two appointments
   _____

Divide these two words into syllables.

3. amusement _____ envelope _____

Who might be saying this?

4. May I see your driver's licence, please? _____

5. Would you like boxes or bags for your items? _____

WEEK **30**
ACTIVITY **4**
TOTAL **/5**

Decide if the underlined parts have a *capitalization error*, a *punctuation error*, a *spelling error* or *no mistake*.

WEEK 30
ACTIVITY 5
TOTAL /5

1. Does it surprise you to know that <u>Canada has six time zones</u> _____

2. The provinces and <u>territorys</u> are divided from west to east. _____

3. The time zones are <u>Pacific Mountain Central Eastern and Atlantic</u> _____

4. <u>newfoundland</u> has its own special time zone. _____

5. Remember the time zones <u>when you want to telephone someone who lives far away.</u> _____

Name: _____

Bonus Activity: Synonyms and Antonyms

WEEK 30

Read the first word in the row. Then read the next three words.

If the word is:
- an *antonym*, colour the box yellow
- a *synonym*, colour the box orange

warmth	cold	heat	chilly
allow	permit	forbid	let
circular	square	round	rectangular
fierce	gentle	dangerous	cruel
amazing	terrific	fabulous	ordinary
faint	dim	weak	strong

MY CANADA — A fellow named Harry Colebourne bought a black bear in White River, Ontario. That bear later became the inspiration for A.A. Milne's *Winnie the Pooh*.

Name: _____

Write the possessive nouns.

1. the purse of the lady   _____

2. the tools of the men   _____

Correct these sentences.

3. hour trip will began on aug 1 2015 and end on aug 21 2015
   _____

4. after it ranged fore times marc finally answered hims sellphone
   _____

Fact or opinion?

5. All girls look great with long hair.   _____

WEEK **31**

ACTIVITY **1**

TOTAL **/5**

Name: _____

What part of speech is the underlined word in these sentences?

1. The marbles <u>scattered</u> all over the table.   _____

2. You will be in <u>scrious</u> trouble if you don't finish your chores.   _____

Correct these sentences.

3. nolan are calling his friend tim to sea if he am ready to play socceer
   _____

4. the house shaked the lights flickered and my sister screamed it was a earthquake
   _____

Write three words that rhyme with "under".

5. _____

WEEK **31**

ACTIVITY **2**

TOTAL **/5**

Name: _____

Underline the prepositional phrases in these sentence

1. Hang your painting on that wall, please.

2. Help your mother with her groceries, Hank.

Present, past or *future*?

3. Time will tell if you are correct. _____

Correct these sentences.

4. come hear zoe and lets me brush yore hare befor school

5. my cousins name is john michael paulson jr

WEEK **31**

ACTIVIT **3**

TOTAL /5

Name: _____

What type of job is being described below?

1. He needs a quick horse when he is trying to rope a calf. _____

Correct these sentences.

2. has you went to male that package to grandma marg yet

3. was you there when paddy sung when irish eyes is smiling

Underline the part of the sentence to match the word.

4. The farmer harvested his crop of hay in four days.   ***Predicate***

5. His livestock will have plenty to eat this winter.   ***Subject***

WEEK **31**

ACTIVIT **4**

TOTAL /5

Name: _____

Explain the meaning of the underlined figures of speech.

1. I love ice cream! I could eat it until the cows come home.
   _____

2. This play is as exciting as watching paint dry.
   _____

3. My dad's favourite saying is, "Time flies when you're having fun."
   _____

4. Do you think someone who turns 50 is over the hill?
   _____

5. My brother and I don't always see eye to eye but we do always help each other.
   _____

WEEK 31

ACTIVITY 5

TOTAL /5

Name: _____

Bonus Activity: Reading Skills

Read the paragraph. Read the sentences. Circle T if the sentence is *true* and F if it is *false*.

Fruits are an important food for us to eat. They contain acids, salts and vitamins that help us maintain a healthy and balanced diet. Even the water and roughage are good for us. Dentists urge us to eat fresh fruit instead of chocolate and candy. If we follow that advice, we are less likely to get holes in our teeth.

1. T F   Fruits are one of the best foods we can eat.
2. T F   A healthy and balanced diet means eating anything we want.
3. T F   If a fruit is really watery, it is bad for us
4. T F   Holes in our teeth are called "cavities".
5. T F   If we eat lots of fruit, we will never get any cavities.

WEEK 31

MY CANADA

Last Mountain Lake Sanctuary in Saskatchewan is North America's oldest bird sanctuary. It was opened in 1887. Each fall, over 450,000 geese stop there during their migration.

Name: _____

Correct these sentences.

1. dew you plan to run agin this year mr mayor asked the reportor

   _____

2. people was scarred when the loin escaped from the woodland zoo

   _____

What do these words have in common?

3. caribou   buffalo   wolf   lynx   coyote _____

Subject pronoun or object pronoun?

4. When will <u>they</u> be arriving?   _____

5. Will you help <u>her</u> with her spelling homework? _____

WEEK 32
ACTIVITY 1
TOTAL /5

Name: _____

Where would the following probably take place?

1. We set up our umbrella and our folding chairs and put on some sunscreen

   _____

Correct these sentences.

2. tanyas birthday is on dec 25 but she selebrates it on dec 24 insteed

   _____

3. kiwis ostriches and penguins cannot fly isnt that strange

   _____

Opinion or *fact*?

4. The life of a Maritime fisherman is the hardest in the world. _____

5. The Grand Banks have long been good fishing grounds. _____

WEEK 32
ACTIVITY 2
TOTAL /5

Name: _____

Circle the cause and underline the effect.

1. I missed the bus because my alarm clock didn't wake me up.

2. He torn his shirt on a branch when he was climbing the tree.

Correct these sentences.

3. most townes have a parade on july 1 to celebrate canadas berthday

_____

4. hour town have a firewerks display wunce it gots vary dark

_____

Write an opinion on this topic: going horseback riding

5. _____

WEEK **32**

ACTIVITY **3**

TOTAL **/5**

Name: _____

Write the pronoun that would replace the underlined words.

1. <u>The three little kittens</u> lost their mittens.

Correct these sentences.

2. the novel the prairie dog conspiracy was wrote by eric wilson

_____

3. the mane character tom austen gots to use his wits to solve the misstery

_____

Complete the analogies.

4. balloon is to light as brick is to _____

5. candy is to sweet as dill pickle is to _____

WEEK **32**

ACTIVITY **4**

TOTAL **/5**

Name: _____

Reference sources: atlas, almanac, dictionary, encyclopedia, thesaurus

What reference source would be best to look for information on the following:

1. to find the meaning of the word "alpine" _____

2. to find the name of the biggest island in the Arctic Ocean _____

3. to find an antonym for "peculiar" _____

4. for information on the work of Parks Canada _____

5. information on how to grow tomatoes _____

WEEK 32
ACTIVITY 5
TOTAL /5

Name: _____

Bonus Activity: A Not-So-Secret Message!

Discover the message by writing the letters in the boxes. Write the letter that comes *before* each one you see. The first one has been done to help you.

I															!
J		b	n		b		q	s	p	v	e		d	b	o	b	e	j	b	o

Write your own personal list of three things that make you proud to be a Canadian.

1. _____

2. _____

3. _____

WEEK 32

MY CANADA — Hartland Covered Bridge in New Brunswick is the longest covered bridge in the world. In 1982, a car hit the bridge and caused $140,000 damage. But... damage to the car was only $400!

ANSWER KEY

WEEK 1: ACTIVITY 1

1. We don't have any snow in our yard yet.
2. My sister, Amy, will say her speech at the Royal Canadian Legion contest
3. fact
4. fiction
5. Catastrophes: great and sudden disasters.

WEEK 1: ACTIVITY 2

1. I don't have any money to buy a treat.
2. I read an amazing adventure story about Vikings visiting North America long ago.
3. One explorer, named Leif the Lucky may have settled in Newfoundland.
4. proper noun
5. common noun

WEEK 1: ACTIVITY 3

1. thesaurus
2. atlas
3. Our family is going to visit the dinosaur display at the Royal Ontario Museum.
4. Wouldn't it be fun to watch whales play in the waters of the Atlantic Ocean?
5. pilot is to airplane as jockey is to horse

WEEK 1: ACTIVITY 4

1. snow – board – ing
2. Fred – er – ic – ton
3. "Have you ever seen a double rainbow in the sky?" asked Alan.
4. I have read most of the adventure books written by Pierre Berton.
5. closing

WEEK 1: ACTIVITY 5

1. She felt confident; was wishing she would win
2. Persuade her
3. Was moving around
4. He has the best ideas; best thinker
5. Started to travel; set off on a journey

BONUS ACTIVITY:

1. British Columbia
2. Ontario
3. Prince Edward Island
4. Alberta
5. Quebec
6. Manitoba
7. Saskatchewan
8. New Brunswick
9. Nova Scotia
10. Newfoundland

WEEK 2: ACTIVITY 1

1. On May 20, 2015, my brother Rick will graduate from McGill University.
2. Are you going to help me with our report on First Nations ceremonies?
3. carried
4. grew, has/have grown
5. antonym

WEEK 2: ACTIVITY 2

1. jumped over the fence with ease
2. Fact
3. Fiction
4. Mom made chocolate chip cookies and we ate them all.
5. "How well did you do on your math test?" Nigel asked.

WEEK 2: ACTIVITY 3

1. remark/mark
2. A team of workers is trying to find treasure on Oak Island.
3. We are reading the poem "The Train Dogs" by E. Pauline Johnson.
4. Canadian treats
5. names of the Great Lakes

Week 2: Activity 4

1. I'm going to Edmonton next week to see my cousin Brady.
2. "Do you think you could ride a horse without a saddle?" asked Rex
3. waist / women / write / <u>wrote</u> / wrong
4. sign / saga / scenery / shoemaker / <u>swim</u>
5. basketball team

Week 2: Activity 5

1. atlas
2. thesaurus
3. atlas, encyclopedia
4. dictionary
5. encyclopedia

Bonus Activity: Just for Fun: Anagrams

1. mane
2. nails
3. spoon
4. bowl
5. bush
6. wasp
7. dawn
8. rock

Week 3: Activity 1

1. "I had mustard, relish, ketchup, and onions on my hot dog," said Connie.
2. This piece of pizza has too much pepperoni and it is too hot to eat.
3. Answers will vary.
4. Answers will vary.
5. fiction

Week 3: Activity 2

1. Car is to street as train is to tracks.
2. Bear is to fur as fish is to scales.
3. We laughed when we heard the story called "How the Bear Got His Short Tail."
4. The Canadian Armed Forces are very brave men and women.
5. Opinion

Week 3: Activity 3

1. Charlottetown, Regina, Edmonton, Toronto: names of provincial capital cities
2. chocolate chip, sugar, gingersnap, wafer: kinds of cookies
3. Before you go to bed, take a bath and brush your teeth.
4. "Don't walk on the clean floor with those dirty boots," said Mom.
5. sink: sank   has/have sunk

Week 3: Activity 4

1. adjective
2. verb
3. We are going to Big Cheese for my birthday party on Saturday.
4. I want to join the Royal Canadian Mounted Police when I am older.
5. Opinion

Week 3: Activity 5

1. We drove our van on a two-hour trip to the city.
2. Danny can run so fast that he wins races all the time and he beats older kids too.
3. When Ellie fell off her bike, she scraped her knee so Mom put a band-aid on it.
4. This store is having a "Going Out of Business Sale" so I want new basketball shoes.
5. Dad is painting my bedroom the green colour I picked.

Bonus Activity: Just for Fun: Rhyming Words

1. boil   2. fish   3. reef   4. soap   5. surf   6. riding

Week 4: Activity 1

1. My parents went to The Golden Dragon for their anniversary.
2. Prof. E. M. Johnson is going to be teaching the course that starts on January 16, 2015.
3. no
4. yes
5. verb

Week 4: Activity 2

1. The <u>ragged little</u> boy was begging for <u>any tiny</u> scrap of food.
2. lives
3. sheep
4. "I'll get you and me an ice cream cone for a treat," said Callie.
5. "Wow! That's a great time for your first run," said Coach Barrett.

Week 4: Activity 3

1. Foot is to sock as head is to hat.
2. Beard is to chin as moustache is to mouth.
3. Don't wait too long to buy your ticket to the big game.
4. Why aren't you going with my brother Eric and me?
5. A ninja breathes <u>softly</u>, moves <u>silently</u> and attacks <u>quickly</u>.

Week 4: Activity 4

1. Object pronoun
2. Object pronoun
3. There are four baby ducks swimming in the pond in the park.
4. Doesn't their mother do a good job of keeping them safe from enemies?
5. P.E.I

Week 4: Activity 5

1. If we play <u>well</u> at the practice today, we may make the team.
2. Jean and <u>I</u> have signed up for Library Helper Club.
3. Did James have a <u>good</u> time on his trip to Vancouver?
4. <u>That</u> apple pie is the best I have ever tasted!
5. Please help <u>her</u> cross the busy street.

Bonus Activity: Antonyms

1. less   2. hard   3. empty   4. under   5. apart
6. outer   7. smooth   8. before   9. cloudy
10. straight   11. backwards   12. dangerous

Week 5: Activity 1

1. Fantasy
2. The scariest book I have ever read is called <u>Into the Dark Waters</u>.
3. Jeffrey hopes to travel to many countries in the world, especially in Asia and Europe.
4. the dresses' colours
5. Duke's truck

Week 5: Activity 2

1. Jack stood <u>beside</u> his brother at the ceremony.
2. They are building a new house <u>near</u> the lake.
3. Children need to be protected against measles, mumps, and chickenpox.
4. "Maddie, will you help me clean out the old attic?" asked Grandma.
5. Answers will vary.

Week 5: Activity 3

1. They were emotional.
2. Don't make a small problem a big one.
3. populate
4. If you don't help him with his math any more, he will get upset.
5. Did their new winter coats all cost the same amount of money?

Week 5: Activity 4

1. Fact
2. The Wilsons asked Noreen to sing at their daughter's wedding in June.
3. Nathan has done his spelling work correctly and so have I.
4. almanac
5. atlas

Week 5: Activity 5

1. Capitalization
2. No mistake
3. Punctuation
4. Capitalization
5. Spelling error

BONUS ACTIVITY: ON THE OPEN SEAS!

1. tanker 2. ship 3. raft 4. canoe 5. yacht
6. cruise ship 7. sailboat 8. submarine

WEEK 6: ACTIVITY 1

1. "Who thinks that Canada owns the North Pole?" asked the teacher.
2. "I thought the polar bears owned it," joked Owen.
3. The <u>cranky old</u> man kept the <u>boy's rubber</u> ball that went through the <u>wire</u> fence.
4. Put the <u>small</u> jars of <u>blueberry</u> jam on the <u>top</u> shelf in the <u>big</u> pantry.
5. Meat that comes from deer

WEEK 6: ACTIVITY 2

1. dusty / dustier / dustiest
2. Preparing to cook something
3. Running a race
4. Jason and he wanted to see the new models at the International Auto Show.
5. Why don't you play quietly while your baby brother, Stewie, is napping?

WEEK 6: ACTIVITY 3

1. Imperative
2. Answers will vary.
3. Answers will vary.
4. Why did those deer come so near to Grampa Bob's cabin?
5. We swam in Lake Ontario seven times in the past year.

WEEK 6: ACTIVITY 4

1. Are we going to go skateboarding with their group on Friday?
2. She and I go for our skating lesson each Tuesday at 3:30.
3. The rider of the horse encouraged it to jump over the highest rail. Common noun
4. Big Ben, a champion jumper, easily cleared the bar. Proper noun
5. Answers will vary.

WEEK 6: ACTIVITY 5

1. I am ready to say it.
2. We will look everywhere.
3. She was very excited and pleased.
4. You make me crazy; give me trouble.
5. A very bad headache.

BONUS ACTIVITY: PREPOSITIONS

1. Frank and Marie went skateboarding <u>in</u> the park.
2. Frank was going too fast and fell <u>off</u> his skateboard.
3. Marie saw what happened and rushed <u>over</u> to help him.
4. Frank wasn't hurt badly, just a few cuts <u>on</u> his legs.
5. Marie walked home <u>with</u> Frank to make him feel better.
6. Frank put his skateboard <u>under</u> his bed.
7. <u>After</u> a few days he decided to try again.

WEEK 7: ACTIVITY 1

1. Claire's dog, Buddy, wags its tail when it likes you.
2. "Do you know who tore the pages of my library book?" asked Chris.
3. swept
4. blew, has/have blown
5. Stranded, shipwrecked

WEEK 7: ACTIVITY 2

1. Answers will vary. Answers need capital letters.
2. Answers will vary. Answers need capital letters.
3. The Arctic; northern Canada
4. It doesn't make any difference if you help me with this boring job.
5. Mom scolded me, " You should have been more careful with your new shoes."

WEEK 7: ACTIVITY 3

1. Subject pronoun
2. You'll need flour, sugar, butter, chocolate chips, and eggs to make those cookies.
3. Do you believe that ice skating is one of the most popular sports in Canada?
4. What kind
5. How many

Week 7: Activity 4

1. Well, you certainly have done a good job on your history project.
2. The fields of golden wheat in Saskatchewan are quite a sight to see.
3. here   quietly   happily   fast
4. rein, reign
5. clause

Week 7: Activity 5

1. encyclopedia
2. encyclopedia
3. thesaurus
4. atlas
5. almanac

Bonus Activity   Teamwork

4 – The food tasted fine but the kitchen was a disaster!
1 – My brother Dan loves to cook.
3. – One night he decided to surprise Mom by cooking dinner.
5 – Mom thanked Dan, looked at me and said, "Join me in the kitchen, Brad?"
2 – Unfortunately, he is not very good at cleaning up his mess.
6 – I'm not good at cooking, but I'm great at helping clean up!

Week 8: Activity 1

1. "Sammy, bring those nails, the hammer, and the screwdriver," said Dad.
2. Did you know that Amelia Earhart was the first woman to fly a plane in Newfoundland?
3. there is
4. he had/would
5. 3:00

Week 8: Activity 2

1. Salutation, greeting, opening
2. closing
3. November
4. Pioneers used oxen held together with a wooden yoke.
5. Their log cabins were often cold and damp during the long winter months.

Week 8: Activity 3

1. proper noun
2. common noun
3. Do you know that Apple Day is a popular fundraiser for Boy Scouts?
4. Canadian explorers like Jacques Cartier and Samuel de Champlain faced many dangers.
5. exclamatory

Week 8: Activity 4

1. Can you help her solve this serious problem with her car?
2. Thanks, Penny, for cleaning up that big mess they made.
3. trans – por – ta – tion
4. freedom
5. clue

Week 8: Activity 5

1. We gave Mom a heart – shaped box of candy for Valentine's Day.
2. During a fierce thunder storm yesterday, lightning struck his barn and it burned down.
3. Watch those icy patches on the sidewalk because you might slip and break some bones.
4. The little kids played a board game called Candyland all afternoon.
5. When Dad and I went camping to Sand Lake Park, we slept in a tent.

Bonus Activity: Are You a Happy Camper?

Answers will vary.

Week 9: Activity 1

1. antic
2. tough
3. Canada's First Nations people were the first people to travel by canoe.
4. Early explorers didn't trust canoes so they hired First Nations guides.
5. Circled: The children

Week 9: Activity 2

1. acter
2. simile
3. Object pronoun
4. Those actors performed so well that the play was a success.
5. "Who's ready for a big adventure?" shouted my funny Uncle Benny.

Week 9: Activity 3

1. settle
2. Prairie dogs are furry little rodents found mainly in Saskatchewan.
3. They live in prairie dog towns that are divided into smaller neighbourhoods.
4. Blvd.
5. Ave.

Week 9: Activity 4

1. Canada's far north is filled with mountains, wilderness, and deep canyons.
2. If you're lucky, you'll see a iceberg as tall as a big city building.
3. All alone, abandoned
4. antonyms
5. synonyms

Week 9: Activity 5

1. All week at the cottage, we <u>caught</u> fish for our dinner.
2. Did you know <u>they're</u> both from Montreal?
3. Is your mother feeling <u>better</u> today?
4. When will <u>their</u> company arrive?
5. Of all the ice cream flavours I've tried, strawberry is the <u>best</u>.

Bonus Activity: Odd Sound Out

1. tub 2. sing 3. made 4. film 5. hate 6. print
7. rule 8. lost

Week 10: Activity 1

1. pronoun
2. adjective
3. The Underground Railway was a secret network of people.
4. Slaves from United States escaped with help from Harriet Tubman.
5. ca'nt

Week 10: Activity 2

1. unemotional
2. encouraged/discouraged; encouraging/discouraging; encouragement
3. Yukon
4. Let's meet Confederation Park for a Picnic with Shirley and Sid.
5. "I will bring apples, juice, and cookies, if you like," I said.

Week 10: Activity 3

1. Preposition
2. "I'm going to clean you room and put things away," said the babysitter.
3. "Don't put my toys away where I can't find them," whined the little boy.
4. 10:30
5. Take these foods:

Week 10: Activity 4

1. They
2. her
3. We don't have time to finish this job but we'll do it tomorrow.
4. An animal came into our garage and tore open our garbage.
5. Answers will vary.

Week 10: Activity 5

1. capitalization
2. No mistake
3. spelling
4. punctuation
5. punctuation

Bonus Activity: Synonyms

1. halt
2. evil
3. damp
4. weak
5. boast
6. entire
7. simple
8. plenty

Week 11: Activity 1

1. Don't walk through those snow angels that Curtis and Sharon made.
2. David, Juan, and Carla are going to Cranbrook, British Columbia for Easter.
3. Singular
4. singular
5. Past

Week 11: Activity 2

1. Clown is to funny as ghost is to scary.
2. Highway is to wide as path is to narrow.
3. Paul said, "Jackie, will you help me with this math problem?"
4. Alice's cat, Sunshine, stuck its nose into the bowl and tried to catch the goldfish.
5. Take advantage of the good weather

Week 11: Activity 3

1. Canada's first prime minister was Sir John A. Macdonald.
2. In 1816, he came to Canada with his parents and lived in Kingston, Ontario.
3. lonely / lonelier / loneliest
4. busy / busier / busiest
5. Interfering

Week 11: Activity 4

1. Fact
2. Fiction
3. Before starting her day, Mrs. Jackson jogs eight kilometres down the road.
4. On Aug. 21, I am having my birthday party at Parkwood Beach.
5. Simile

Week 11: Activity 5

1. dictionary
2. atlas
3. thesaurus
4. encyclopedia
5. almanac

Bonus Activity: Creative Compounds

Sentences and illustrations will vary.

Week 12: Activity 1

1. Metaphor
2. Did you read the article called "Canoeing in Canada" in Canadian Geographic?
3. Mr. Connell, my neighbour, has taught in Manitoba, Alberta, and Ontario.
4. how   5. where

Week 12: Activity 2

1. She and I were paid fourteen dollars to babysit two children on Saturday.
2. The Baytown Animal Shelter doesn't have any more room for rescued cats .
3. Answers will vary.
4. Answers will vary.
5. Opinion

Week 12: Activity 3

1. Mr. Evans' class planted trees in Lyndhill Park on Earth Day last year.
2. Go, team, go!" screamed the excited fans at the World Cup Game.
3. fortune
4. courage
5. crispy, fresh, toasted

Week 12: Activity 4

1. The campers were afraid when they heard the howling of the wolves.
2. "Mom, do I really have to give the dog a bath?" complained Alex.
3. Past
4. Future
5. Proper noun

Week 12: Activity 5

1. Eli wanted to play ball with his friends but he had to clean his room first.
2. We loved the hamburgers that Dad barbequed for our lunch.
3. My dog hurt its leg so we took her to our vet, Dr. Willows.
4. The cows were mooing because they were hungry so the farmer put them in the pasture.
5. Our school team was proud that they won the championship because they played their best.

Bonus Activity: Action Analogies

1. Run is to horse as swim is to <u>fish</u>.
2. Sniff is to nose as wink is to <u>eye</u>.
3. Talk is to person as quack is to <u>duck</u>.
4. See is to eye as hear is to <u>ear</u>.
5. Touch is to finger as smell is to <u>nose</u>.
6. Paint is to brush as draw is to <u>pencil</u>.

Week 13: Activity 1

1. <u>Cookies, cupcakes and muffins</u> are on sale today.
2. Don't you understand that we have too many jobs to do before Monday?
3. Charlene had to sing "The Maple Leaf Forever" at the ceremony.
4. Make some tea <u>in that new teapot</u>.
5. The secretary takes messages <u>for her boss</u>.

Week 13: Activity 2

1. ref – er – ee   bad – min – ton
2. correctly: suffix   unknown: prefix
3. Would you like to play Scrabble or do you want to play Monopoly?
4. My brother, Eddy, ate my cookies, muffin, and drank my milk.
5. My pet hamster, Angel, <u>does funny tricks</u>.

Week 13: Activity 3

1. Preposition
2. When I lent you my baseball I thought you would return it.
3. Our uniforms got dirty from playing on that muddy field.
4. How many
5. What kind

Week 13: Activity 4

1. Answers will vary.
2. I read <u>Storm Fear</u> before I went to sleep last night.
3. "Did you knit those mitts all by yourself?" asked Mrs. Blair.
4. dives   diving   diver
5. marries   married   marrying   marriage

Week 13: Activity 5

1. That was the <u>scariest</u> movie I have ever seen.
2. Everyone <u>tried</u> to catch the string of the runaway kite.
3. Harry is the <u>oldest</u> child in his family.
4. Was that math test the <u>most difficult</u> you have ever taken?
5. You always finish your work <u>faster</u> than your brother.

Bonus Activity: Plenty of Prefixes

1. rewrite
2. unfair
3. unlucky
4. recover
5. retry
6. uncommon
7. unhealthy
8. refill

Week 14: Activity 1

1. Mike broke our window but it was an accident and he paid to have it fixed.
2. Wait for the referee to blow the whistle before you start to play .
3. Constant and lasting forever
4. fortune
5. become

Week 14: Activity 2

1. Dr. Ashton, my dentist, is always very gentle with her patients.
2. Why are Lee and Stella digging holes in their backyard?
3. nervous, scared, upset
4. hard
5. Opinion

Week 14: Activity 3

1. who is
2. they have
3. We asked Mom, "Can we play outside in the rain?"
4. Polar Bear National Park is on the shores of Hudson Bay and James Bay.
5. Verb

Week 14: Activity 4

1. Odessa is wearing a red sweater, blue pants and her new black shoes .
2. "Children of the Wind" by Carl Sandburg is a poem about two purple martins.
3. holiday
4. prime minister
5. Carpenter / Handyman

Week 14: Activity 5

1. Capitalization
2. Punctuation
3. No mistake
4. Spelling
5. Punctuation

Bonus Activity: Sailors and Ships

1. harbour 2. seafarer 3. tugboat 4. bunk
5. captain 6. rudder 7. ferry 8. yacht 9. fleet
10. stern 11. funnel 12. oar

Week 15: Activity 1

1. Present
2. Future
3. Circled: Sat.
4. "Do your friends prefer video games or board games?" asked Ralph.
5. Sailing long ago was very dangerous even for adventurous sailors

Week 15: Activity 2

1. They
2. Canadian animals that appear on coins.
3. Do you think it was a good idea to change one and two dollar bills into coins?
4. antonyms
5. synonyms

Week 15: Activity 3

1. tomatoes
2. in – flu – ence
3. com – mu – ni – ca – tion
4. When you press the button, the elevator will start.
5. "Neither he nor I are going to volunteer for those jobs," said Ian.

Week 15: Activity 4

1. Fact
2. Fiction
3. Have you ever been skiing in Banff National Park?
4. You would needs to obey the rules and listen to the advice of the Ski Patrol.
5. 2 relax 3 release 1 rejoice 5 relieve 4 reliable

Week 15: Activity 5

1. Mr. Seaman is the oldest person in our town.
2. That mall is busy every day of the week.
3. Your drawings are the best.
4. Put that medicine on the highest shelf.
5. If you do that, it will make Dad angry.

Bonus Activity: Prepare to Punctuate!

1. Jenny's birthday is in January.
2. May I go to the playground?
3. The Queen Mary sailed across the Atlantic.
4. Have you ever been on a cruise ship?
5. We shop at Loblaws and Foodland.
6. I had fun at Sally's party!
7. Why were you so late, Susan?
8. How old is Robert Brown?

Week 16: Activity 1

1. Be very slow
2. Pronoun
3. Preposition
4. Our Aunt Lorraine is getting married on Labour Day weekend.
5. Mr. Edwards, the custodian, moved those students desk in Miss Hart's room.

Week 16: Activity 2

1. Answers will vary.
2. How
3. When
4. Could you bring a large, cold, juicy watermelon to the Sunday School picnic?
5. An old elm tree fell across our road and blocked our way.

Week 16: Activity 3

1. Exclamatory
2. Imperative
3. Answers will vary.
4. Do you believe that cars will drive themselves in the future?
5. Will I read Into the North or Lost in the Rockies for my book report?

Week 14: Activity 4

1. Put your coat, mitts, hat, and scarf in that closet.
2. What time are we due at the Grand Theatre for the play Thumbelina?
3. hockey player
4. river
5. P.S.

Week 16: Activity 5

1. My cousin Hank wants to be a cowboy and ride a horse.
2. Hank wants to live on a ranch so he can herd and rope cattle.
3. This summer he is going to Alberta to his grandfather's huge ranch.
4. He wants to learn to trot and gallop and ride fast.
5. He might get to round up wild horses which would be hard work.

Bonus Activity: Bundle Up! Word Search

	s	n	o	w	p	a	n	t	s			
	w		c									
	e	o										
	a				b							
t	t	l	e	g	w	a	r	m	e	r	s	
	e				l			i				
	r			s	a				t			
					c					t		
s	t	o	o	b	l	a				o	e	
					a		r			q	n	
			g	l	o	v	e	s	f	u		s
					a					e		

Week 17: Activity 1

1. By the end of March, our class will finish its study of the Klondike Gold Rush.
2. When we heard about the bad weather in Quebec, we cancelled our ski trip.
3. un – pleas – ant
4. sharp – en – er
5. Everyone screamed as the roller coaster went faster and faster. Amusement Park, Country Fair

Week 17: Activity 2

1. Nature: what kind
2. First: which one
3. Jane, the lifeguard, waved the flag to warn the swimmers of the storm.
4. When Phil sends me his new email address, I will write him a message.
5. Lieut.

Week 17: Activity 3

1. noun
2. adverb
3. Answers will vary.
4. "Why can't Aiden and Art ever get to our game on time?" asked Brad.
5. The wind blew so hard that our big maple tree lost some big branches.

Week 17: Activity 4

1. Fact
2. Fiction
3. The Travelling Theatre Players are coming to our school to perform <u>Rumplestiltskin</u>.
4. "Has you ever heard the song called "This Old Man?" asked the kindergarten teacher.
5. Subject

Week 17: Activity 5

1. She is a very good swimmer.
2. Thinking really hard about it.
3. Not thinking straight or using common sense.
4. Overweight, chubby
5. Can't stop thinking about it.

Bonus Activity: Homophone Analogies

1. Ate is to eight as beat is to <u>beet</u>.
2. Hear is to here as as deer is to <u>dear</u>.
3. Cent is to sent as hair is to <u>hare</u>.
4. Pair is to pear as sail is to <u>sale</u>.
5. Right is to write as rode is to <u>road</u>.
6. Steal is to steel as meat is to <u>meet</u>.
7. Sea is to sea as heard is to <u>herd</u>.
8. Their is to there as stair is to <u>stare</u>.

Week 18: Activity 1

1. oxen
2. foxes
3. Canada trades lumber, oil, fish, and wheat to country's around the world.
4. We have to protect our natural resources for future generations.
5. booth   forsooth   truth   Ruth

Week 18: Activity 2

1. Words were very hurtful, mean.
2. The car was not any good; didn't run properly.
3. Mom likes to sing lullabies like "Rock a Bye Baby" to my baby sister Pam.
4. Because my sister Pauline and I were born on the same day, we have one big party.
5. communication

Week 18: Activity 3

1. Dr. and Mr. Briggs are excited about their vacation plans to go to Vancouver.
2. Bill doesn't need any help with his homework assignment.
3. Past
4. Future
5. plural

Week 18: Activity 4

1. Interrogative
2. Were the actors nervous before the play began?
3. Milly picked an apple from our tree and then she took a big bite.
4. At a lake, river, stream
5. Supermarket

Week 18: Activity 5

1. dictionary
2. encyclopedia
3. encyclopedia
4. thesaurus
5. atlas

Bonus Activity: Sounds Like ...

1. Horses <u>neigh</u>.
2. Ducks <u>quack</u>.
3. Hens <u>cluck</u>.
4. Lions <u>roar</u>.
5. Bees <u>buzz</u>.
6. Mice <u>squeak</u>.
7. Roosters <u>crow</u>.
8. Doors <u>slam</u>.
9. Chains <u>jangle</u>.
10. Sparrows <u>chirp</u>.
11. Dogs <u>bark</u>.
12. Horns <u>honk</u>.

Week 19: Activity 1

1. The mother wolf has eight, furry, chubby pups in her litter.
2. All people, animals, and plants need fresh clean water to live.
3. <u>Aren't</u> you finished eating your lunch yet?
4. synonym: difficult, solid; antonym: easy, unsteady
5. synonym: cold, frigid; antonym: warm

Week 19: Activity 2

1. ostrich
2. "Look out!" he called. "The tree branch is falling near you!"
3. Marty saw an animal dig into the garbage bag last night.
4. Past   5. Future

Week 19: Activity 3

1. Prof.
2. Subject
3. Predicate
4. Luke ate most of his hot dog but he left some of the bun.
5. Do you have the phone number for Chubby Chicken Take-out on Main Street?

Week 19: Activity 4

1. in – ter – sec – tion
2. pro – por – tion
3. them
4. "After you are done your chores, you may play outside," said Mom.
5. I may try out for the soccer team or I may join track and field.

Week 19: Activity 5

1. The little children sang and danced in the play while the parents watched them.
2. Grandpa grows corn, tomatoes, and beans in his big garden.
3. My Aunt Mel has lived in New Brunswick for 10 years.
4. Today will be a snow day for us because there was a big snowstorm last night.
5. Fifteen people entered our school talent contest and Sarah won with her magic act.

Bonus Activity: Reading Skills

1. b) Anna enjoyed building her plane.
2. c) pink and green.
3. a) The Best Birthday Present

Week 20: Activity 1

1. Jr.
2. He is a good gardener; can make things grow well.
3. Loony, silly, not sensible
4. "Is this what you were looking for?" asked the saleslady.
5. My friends threw me a surprise birthday party last Saturday night.

Week 20: Activity 2

1. "Don't touch that red hot pan on the stove!" warned Allan.
2. Ari likes to read folk tales about talking animals and unusual places.
3. ob – li – ga – tion
4. nev – er – the – less
5. Circled: because I get sick easily.

Week 20: Activity 3

1. detect
2. Devin said, "I hope he chooses me to be on his team."
3. Sometimes he feels like going outside and sometimes he doesn't.
4. Aim <u>accurately</u>, shoot <u>straight</u> and you may hit the target.
5. The wolf huffed <u>loudly</u>, puffed <u>strongly</u> and cheered <u>gleefully</u> when the house fell <u>down</u>.

Week 20: Activity 4

1. most, post, boast, coast, roast, toast
2. bone, drone, phone, lone, tone, moan, loan,
3. We're leaving for Calgary tonight on Air Canada's 6 o'clock flight.
4. My aunt and uncle will meet us at the airport at 9 o'clock sharp.
5. wagon

Week 20: Activity 5

1. My sister Esther looked so beautiful as she walked down the aisle.
2. Her pet rabbit ate a whole head of lettuce yesterday.
3. How much profit is there in cutting grass in your neighbourhood?
4. The scent of that perfume is very strong.
5. How many patients does your dentist have?

Bonus Activity: It's a Date

1. Dec. 31, (year will vary)
2. Dec. 25, (year will vary)
3. answers will vary
4. answers will vary
5. answers will vary
6. answers will vary

Week 21: Activity 1

1. Stop talking
2. Does everything she can
3. "Don't forgot to feed and water the dog before you go to school," reminded Dad.
4. The view from the mountain doesn't look like anything I've ever seen before.
5. Jeremy's new boots

Week 21: Activity 2

1. Frogs, snakes, and water bugs live in our pond in the backyard.
2. We always go to the beach when the weather is so hot.
3. suffix
4. prefix
5. unique, unusual: synonyms

Week 21: Activity 3

1. at the airport
2. Seth is spending August at his grandparents' cottage in the Muskokas.
3. Will you help us build a snow fort in Bridwell Park on Sunday?
4. Possessive
5. Subject

Week 21: Activity 4

1. Those stories that our camp counsellor told were really scary.
2. Have you ever gone water-skiing on Lake Winnipeg?
3. lucky / luckier / luckiest
4. crazy / crazier / craziest
5. blouse / grouse / louse / mouse

Week 21: Activity 5

1. Capitalization
2. Punctuation
3. No mistake
4. Spelling
5. Capitalization

Bonus Activity: Know Your Fruits and Veggies!

1. a red fruit for salads tomato
2. can be used to make pie pumpkin
3. long yellow fruit banana
4. red vegetable with a hot taste radish
5. can be used to make pickles cucumber
6. can be yellow, green or red apple
7. ears of corn
8. has sour juice lemon
9. grows under the ground potato
10. leaf used in salad lettuce
11. very large fruit watermelon
12. sweet, dried grape raisin

Week 22: Activity 1

1. He found his slipper under the couch.
2. We threw the ball high into the air.
3. Any colour word could be an answer.
4. Have you ridden on a paddle boat on King's Lake yet?
5. Linda shouted, "Look a double rainbow! I've never seen one before."

Week 22: Activity 2

1. bare dare fare glare hare hair lair stare stair
2. They   3. him
4. Michelle, Maggie, and Lucy are coming to my house for Sunday dinner.
5. "The whole team is going to Pizza Palace after the game," said Coach Wills.

Week 22: Activity 3

1. dinosaur
2. holiday
3. semicircle   motorcycle
4. I can see that we'll have those little kids rebuild their snowman.
5. Jim and I were excited about running in the Terry Fox Marathon of Hope.

Week 22: Activity 4

1. Conservation officer, game warden, park ranger
2. Their goalie broke his ankle and now he can't play hockey with the team.
3. "Let's have an adventure in that gloomy cave," said Andy.
4. If you stay until the end of the play, you will see the grand finale. The showcase ending
5. Not regular; misshapen; odd

Week 22: Activity 5

1. difficult task; hard to do
2. Very quiet; silent
3. Don't count on something until you know it is for certain.
4. A great deal of money
5. A very bad headache

Bonus Activity: Colourful Parts of Speech.

Nouns: red : mouse, mole, skunk, chipmunk, squirrel, rabbit
Adjectives: green : grey, busy, timid sassy, lively, bold
Verbs: blue : dash, spray, scurry, dig, squeak, hide
Adverbs: orange : loudly, rapidly, furiously, softly, quickly, secretly

Week 23: Activity 1

1. They heard thunder, saw lightning, and felt rain during the storm.
2. What happened here? This whole house is one big mess!
3. A small tower on a building
4. Add any school subject.
5. Add any holiday.

Week 23: Activity 2

1. "Wow! What a great looking sports car!" exclaimed Hal.
2. Speak softly because we don't want anybody to hear our secret.
3. Future   4. Past   5. Body

Week 23: Activity 3

1. Pete yelled to warn Kevin but it was too late.
2. Our team will play at 2 o'clock sharp at Cook's Arena.
3. synonyms
4. di – lap – i – dat – ed
5. in – no – cent

Week 23: Activity 4

1. heading   2. knife   3. baby
4. "Stopping by Woods on a Snowy Evening" by Robert Frost is a well known poem.
5. The family that lived next door went to another city to live.

Week 23: Activity 5

1. atlas
2. almanac
3. atlas
4. encyclopedia
5. thesaurus

Bonus Activity: Wild Weather !

1. frost   2. smog   3. lightning   4. rain   5. thunder
6. fog   7. hail   8. blizzard   9. gale   10. drizzle

Week 24: Activity 1

1. A piece of cloth or paper used for wiping your lips and fingers
2. After digging for two hours, those men were covered with dirt.
3. Did your sister promise to arrive by 7 o'clock for the meeting?
4. a boulder is heavy, a pebble is light
5. a shout is loud, a whisper is quiet/soft

Week 24: Activity 2

1. Fact
2. Opinion
3. Both boys' bikes were red with blue racing stripes.
4. We have sailed on Uncle Fred's sailboat at least eight times.
5. Imperative

Week 24: Activity 3

1. antonym
2. Cody's friends were afraid of the dark so his mom gave them a flashlight.
3. Those greedy boys drank all the cold milk we had.
4. She
5. It

Week 24: Activity 4

1. "Have you ever read the Kids' Almanac?" asked Jake.
2. We all sang "Happy Birthday" before Roxanne cut the cake.
3. common noun
4. proper noun
5. Adverb

Week 24: Activity 5

1. One hot day, we bought ice cream cones to eat while we sat on the park bench.
2. Our teacher read us three funny poems today.
3. As the fans watched the ball game, they cheered for the home team and the home team won.
4. My brother ate the last six cookies so now the cookie jar is empty.
5. As we walked along the crowded street, looking in shop windows, we saw puppies.

Bonus Activity: The Great Canadian Scramble

1. Rocky Mountains
2. Niagara Falls
3. Peggy's Cove
4. Hartland Covered Bridge
5. Perce Rock

Week 25: Activity 1

1. "Are those Sally's favourite red shoes?" asked Daisy.
2. Callie did the cooking and cleaning to surprise her mother.
3. We are going swimming <u>tomorrow</u>.
4. Stand <u>straight</u> and I will measure you.
5. I had

Week 25: Activity 2

1. "You aren't the boss of me!" yelled the naughty little boy.
2. Jonah leaped on his snowboard and sailed down the mountain.
3. Future
4. Medicine Hat: 4
5. Portage la Prairie: 5

Week 25: Activity 3

1. Simile
2. Metaphor
3. Spot's tail wagged as I gave him the baby's leftovers.
4. When will the technician, Mr. Carrell, fix our computer?
5. 4 morsel   5 mortal   1 moral   2 more   3 morning

Week 25: Activity 4

1. "What do you like on your burger and hot dog?" asked Max.
2. Those terrible winds blew an umbrella and chair right off our deck.
3. disappearance , disappeared, disappearing, reappearance, reappeared, reappearing
4. Fantasy
5. Fact

Week 25: Activity 5

1. How many baby <u>bunnies</u> were born to your pet rabbit?
2. Please give a cup of hot chocolate to <u>him</u>.
3. <u>Who's</u> going hiking with you?
4. My brother <u>was</u> married in 2000.
5. When <u>do</u> you need a ride to school?

Teacher Notes

BONUS ACTIVITY: READING SKILLS

1. F   2. T   3. T   4. F

WEEK 26: ACTIVITY 1

1. She is very kind and generous.
2. He has a sore throat, can't speak clearly.
3. Prof. Lewis ordered those special specimens of exotic insects, didn't he?
4. The boys were hungry, tired, and dirty after helping us build the tree house.
5. on

WEEK 26: ACTIVITY 2

1. jump/leap/hop
2. sad/unhappy
3. who will
4. Did you know in February snow fell every day in the Maritimes?
5. The Athens Figure Skating Club is the best in the area, don't you agree?

WEEK 26: ACTIVITY 3

1. plural possessive
2. singular possessive
3. "How many pieces of pumpkin pie did Tony eat?" asked Julie.
4. Those boys are going to be in trouble for walking on Ann's floor with their dirty boots.
5. satisfy   satisfied   will satisfy

WEEK 26: ACTIVITY 4

1. "Why don't people make homemade ice cream today?" inquired Jessica.
2. Those kids all chose Junior Scrabble as their favourite board game to play.
3. A fair, carnival or amusement park
4. Flu shot clinic, doctor's office
5. appoint

WEEK 26: ACTIVITY 5

1. Capitalization
2. Spelling
3. Punctuation
4. No mistake
5. Punctuation

BONUS ACTIVITY: USING A THESAURUS

1. Synonym: gloomy, black, shadowy;
   Antonym: light, happy, bright
2. Synonym: beautiful, elegant, flowing
   Antonym: awkward, clumsy, gawky
3. Synonym: chance, fate, karma
   Antonym: hardship, misfortune, distress
4. Synonym: comrade, companion, friend
   Antonym: stranger, enemy, foe
5. Synonym: remain, rest, wait
   Antonym: hasten, go, depart, leave

WEEK 27: ACTIVITY 1

1. They have gone shopping for soccer socks, shorts, cleats, and headbands.
2. Their favourite story is <u>I Want That Dog</u> by Jean Little.
3. Predicate
4. Subject
5. Answers will vary.

WEEK 27: ACTIVITY 2

1. Exclamatory
2. Imperative
3. atmosphere   3
4. They have moved to a new apartment at 666 South Street in Calgary.
5. After the seeds sprouted into little plants, they grew quickly in one week.

WEEK 27: ACTIVITY 3

1. A platform used to hold workers while they work on a building.
2. Give importance or special attention to something
3. You mustn't leave the house while your parents are gone shopping.
4. Uncle Fred bought us fries, Pogos, tacos, and wraps for Ben's party.
5. 1 crocodile   3 croquet   4 crossbow   2 crocus
   5 crouch

Week 27: Activity 4

1. nose, pose, froze, doze, toes, blows, grows, flows,
2. Are we supposed to read the chapter on Henry Hudson or on Martin Frobisher?
3. The explorers who tried to find the Northwest Passage were very brave.
4. What kind, which one
5. What kind

Week 27: Activity 5

1. From the actual source.
2. Someone who has a big vocabulary.
3. Nothing moved
4. Annoying me
5. He had a big smile on his face.

Bonus Activity: Maple Goodness

d	e	l	i	c	i	o	u	s	l	s
	t					a	y	i	p	t
	r			p		r	o	i		e
g	a	t	h	e	r		u	b	g	e
	c		m	a	p	l	e	p	o	w
	t			b	u	c	k	e	t	s
	o		o					s		
	r	p	i	p	e	l	i	n	e	s

Week 28: Activity 1

1. Bom – bar – di – er
2. snow – mo – bile
3. I can't ever decide which I like best—skiing or tobogganing.
4. Because I broke my leg, I missed two birthday parties.
5. forgot

Week 28: Activity 2

1. At a graduation ceremony
2. Derek will need a new brake on his bike before he'll be able to race.
3. Those little kids got wet from wading in those puddles and splashing each another.
4. Fiction
5. Fact

Week 28: Activity 3

1. How, to what extent
2. Where
3. Does your <u>elderly</u> uncle still drive that <u>old</u> John Deere tractor?
4. Did you see <u>Lost Mines of the North</u> on television last night?
5. Dad blew a tire when he hit a large pothole in the road on Tuesday.

Week 28: Activity 4

1. Mon . Aug. 21, 2007.
2. We are leaving for the Canadian Museum of Civilization at 8 o'clock sharp tomorrow.
3. Events at the Calgary Stampede include bull riding, roping, barrel racing, and bronc riding.
4. At an airport.
5. Automotive plant

Week 28: Activity 5

1. encyclopedia
2. encyclopedia
3. thesaurus
4. almanac
5. atlas

Bonus Activity: Just for Fun: Anagrams

2. owl; A bird that hunts at night
3. lake; body of fresh water
4. saw; A tool for cutting
5. pals; Friends
6. loot; Money, treasure

Week 29: Activity 1

1. We climbed to the top of Rock Dunder. What an amazing view!
2. If Gabe strikes out this time, we will lose the final game.
3. singular, plural
4. plural
5. ease, tease, squeeze, freeze, fleas/flees, knees, bees,

Teacher Notes

WEEK 29: ACTIVITY 2

1. Did you know that Alexander Graham Bell was co – inventor of the first hydrofoil?
2. He also made the first one-way long-distance telephone call between two towns in Ontario.
3. Someone who goes with you, a friend
4. Limped, walked unsteadily
5. Exclamatory

WEEK 29: ACTIVITY 3

1. You have to work really hard to beat my friend, Jerry.
2. Mrs. Hart, the school secretary, is very polite to all visitors.
3. common noun
4. proper noun
5. that, little, brown, furry

WEEK 29: ACTIVITY 4

1. populate
2. regard
3. Their mom is looking for a new job at Bayside Library in Fort William
4. When I was a little girl, we lived in Brandon, Manitoba.
5. tem – per – a – ture

WEEK 29: ACTIVITY 5

1. He threw that tiny fish back into the lake.
2. Mike was bringing the marshmallows for our campfire treat.
3. Someone needs to collect some wood for our campfire.
4. Remember to invite Cameron and his cousin, Carter.
5. We might stay for two nights if our parents agree.

BONUS ACTIVITY: GENERAL STORE GOODS UNSCRAMBLE

1. oodf: food
2. lcothnig: clothing
3. nugs: guns
4. oslot: tools
5. srpeapewns: newspapers
6. soty: toys
7. numaitimon: ammunition
8. libnugid eritamals: building materials

WEEK 30: ACTIVITY 1

1. Any freshwater body of water.
2. Each Saturday at 10:00, my little sister watches "Strawberry Shortcake" on television.
3. I am reading one chapter of Holes every night before I go to sleep.
4. interior
5. camera

WEEK 30: ACTIVITY 2

1. Opinion
2. Our grandparents took both families to the Golden Dragon to celebrate.
3. After working for eight hours, Caleb and Ryan finished the rail fence.
4. adjective
5. noun

WEEK 30: ACTIVITY 3

1. Reva bought her favourite book, Red Fern, at Book Traders on King Street.
2. Paula, may I stay with you in your cabin at Kid Camp this summer?
3. went / have gone , will go
4. 3 elegant   2 elbow   5 elf   1 elastic   4 elephant
5. 1 post   3 postal   2 postage   4 post card   5 post office

Teacher Notes

WEEK 30: ACTIVITY 4

1. "The circus is in town!" yelled Tammy. "I see the monkeys in that truck."
2. Every day people hurry to work, to school, to shop, and to appointments.
3. a – muse – ment   en – ve – lope
4. Police officer
5. Cashier or bagger in a supermarket

WEEK 30: ACTIVITY 5

1. punctuation
2. spelling
3. punctuation
4. capitalization
5. No mistake

BONUS ACTIVITY: SYNONYMS AND ANTONYMS

1. yellow, orange, yellow
2. orange, yellow, orange
3. yellow orange, yellow
4. ellow, orange, orange
5. orange, orange, yellow
6. orange, orange, yellow

WEEK 31: ACTIVITY 1

1. the lady's purse
2. the men's tools
3. Our trip will begin on Aug. 1, 2015, and end on Aug. 21, 2015.
4. After it rang four times, Marc finally answered his cellphone.
5. Opinion

WEEK 31: ACTIVITY 2

1. Verb
2. Adjective
3. Nolan is calling his friend, Tim, to see if he is ready to play soccer.
4. The house shook, the lights flickered, and my sister screamed it was a earthquake.
5. blunder, wonder, asunder

WEEK 31: ACTIVITY 3

1. Hang your painting on that wall, please.
2. Help your mother with her groceries, Hank.
3. Future
4. Come here, Zoe, and let me brush your hair before school.
5. My cousin's name is John Michael Paulson Jr.

WEEK 31: ACTIVITY 4

1. Cowboy, ranch hand
2. Have you gone to mail that package to Grandma Marg yet?
3. Were you there when Paddy sang "When Irish Eyes Are Smiling"?
4. Predicate
5. Subject

WEEK 31: ACTIVITY 5

1. For a long time, forever.
2. Very dull and boring.
3. Time goes by quickly when you are enjoying what you are doing.
4. Too old to do things
5. Don't always agree on ideas.

BONUS ACTIVITY: READING SKILLS

1. T   2. F   3. F   4. T   5. F

WEEK 32: ACTIVITY 1

1. "Do you plan to run again this year Mr. Mayor?" asked the reporter.
2. People were scared when the lion escaped from the Woodland Zoo.
3. names of Canadian animals
4. subject
5. Object

WEEK 32: ACTIVITY 2

1. At the beach
2. Tanya's birthday is on Dec. 25, but she celebrates it on Dec. 24 instead.
3. Kiwis, ostriches, and penguins cannot fly. Isn't that strange?
4. Opinion
5. Fact

Week 32: Activity 3

1. Circled: because my alarm clock didn't wake me up.
2. Circled: when he was climbing the tree.
3. Most towns have a parade on July 1 to celebrate Canada's birthday.
4. Our town has a fireworks display once it gets very dark.
5. Answers will vary.

Week 32: Activity 4

1. they
2. The novel, The Prairie Dog Conspiracy was written by Eric Wilson.
3. The main character, Tom Austen gets to use his wits to solve the mystery.
4. balloon is to light as brick is to heavy.
5. candy is to sweet as dill pickle is to sour

Week 32: Activity 5

1. dictionary
2. atlas
3. thesaurus
4. encyclopedia
5. almanac

Bonus Activity: A Not-So-Secret Message!

I am a proud Canadian!

www.ingramcontent.com/pod-product-compliance
Lightning Source LLC
Chambersburg PA
CBHW081203240426
43669CB00039B/2800